The Dreamer

By Susan E. Hilliard

Illustrated by Ned O.

STANDARD PUBLISHING
Cincinnati, Ohio   24-03986

Library of Congress Cataloging-in-Publication Data
Hilliard, Susan E.
　The dreamer/Susan E. Hillard.
　　p. cm.—(Decide your own adventure)
　Summary: The reader makes choices about the unfolding of the life of Joseph.
　ISBN 0-87403-726-3
　1. Joseph (Son of Jacob)—Juvenile literature. 2. Bible. O.T—Biography—Juvenile literature. 3. Plot-your-own stories. [1. Joseph (Son of Jacob) 2. Bible stories—O.T. 3. Plot-your-own stories.] I Title. II. Series: Hilliard, Susan E. Decide your own adventure.
BS580.J6H54 1990
222',11092—dc20　　　　　　　　　　　　　　　　　90-33557
　　　　　　　　　　　　　　　　　　　　　　　　　　　CIP
　　　　　　　　　　　　　　　　　　　　　　　　　　　AC

Edited by Theresa C. Hayes

Copyright © 1990 by the
STANDARD PUBLISHING Company, Cincinnati, Ohio.
A Division of STANDEX INTERNATIONAL Corporation.
Printed in U.S.A.

Attention, Reader!

You cannot read this book as you would any other. You are embarking upon a very special journey though time, in search of answers to a quest you are about to receive. On this journey you will travel in a chariot of fire, and you will sometimes be allowed to choose between alternate places or times. The chariot will take you swiftly to the alternative of your choice.

Your first step is to look for a small, parchment scroll in the chariot. This parchment contains the object of your quest.

Next, find and read the larger scroll, which is a vital archive of historical facts that can aid you in making the right choices during your journey.

And now, begin the adventure!

The Chariot

A chariot of fire stands before you. The chariot itself seems solid enough, although it appears to be completely in flames. Your heart thudding, you step closer and notice that the fire is not hot—only pleasantly warm. Through the shimmering flames you see a beautiful horse hitched to the chariot, standing patiently. The quietness of the beast has a calming effect on you, and you find that your heart is not hammering quite so violently. You hesitantly step into the chariot. Nothing happens. You are surrounded by flames, yet nothing is burning. You step farther into the chariot and notice a plain wooden box on the floor. Upon the box is written "Rules for Travel." You open the box.

On the inside of the lid, you read....

Rules for Travel

You must follow these rules on your journey. If you do not, the chariot will return you to the present and you will never be able to complete your quest.

I You may not change history in any way—you are only an observer.
II You may choose only from the alternatives that you are given.
III You may not bring twentieth-century customs, clothing, or equipment with you. Tell no one you may meet of your journey.
IV You may not bring any souvenirs of your journey home with you.

You will find that language differences will not be a problem for you—you will automatically think and speak in the language of your host place and time.

Now you notice a finely-woven, snowy-white garment in the box. As you eagerly pull out fold after fold, a piece of parchment flutters to the floor of the chariot. You pick it up and see a rough sketch of an Egyptian male dressed in a simple pullover shirt tucked into the waist of a knee-length kilt.

Hastily, you remove your twentieth-century clothing and wrap the rectangular kilt securely around your waist. You knot the ends firmly, then pull the shirt over your head and tuck it in at the waist.

Eager to begin the journey, the steed now paws the ground. A thrill of excitement races down your spine! Wadding your discarded clothing into a bundle, you fling it out of the chariot. You drop to your knees and grope anxiously for the parchment scrolls. At last your fingers touch some things in the dark forward corners of the chariot that feel like cylinders of paper. Eagerly, you draw them out.

Anxious to discover your quest, you unroll the smaller scroll and read. . . .

The Quest

You are instructed to go to the time of Joseph, to discover how Joseph was like Daniel, who lived almost 1,400 years later. Why is Joseph sometimes called the foreshadow of the Savior? Why did Joseph's brothers hate him so much?

You remember that Scriptures say that Joseph's brothers were jealous over a special coat given to him by their father. Is that why they hated him so much? You have always wondered if there wasn't more to the story than that!

Eagerly, you unroll the larger scroll and glance through it. On this scroll you find written. . . .

Archives

I. God told Abraham that his descendants would be strangers in a land not their own for four hundred years, that for at least part of that time they would be enslaved and oppressed, and that the fourth generation would lead them back to Canaan. From the time that Abraham first received these promises to the birth of Isaac—the beginning of the fulfillment—was thirty years. From the birth of Isaac to the time when the Israelites left Egypt and received God's law was *four hundred years*, to the day.

II. Joseph was sold into slavery when he was seventeen years old. For the next thirteen years, it appeared as though God had completely forgotten about him—but in *one day* Joseph went from being a prisoner to being the second-in-command under Pharaoh himself.

III. The well-being of the Egyptians depended completely on the Nile river. During inundation, when the Nile flooded, rich black soil was deposited over the land. This soil held enough moisture to produce two crops each year. If the Nile did not rise enough, fewer crops could be grown in a smaller area—and people went hungry. Several years of low inundation resulted in famine and death.

IV. Joseph was sold by his brothers for the price of a slave—at that time, twenty shekels of silver. Almost 2,000 years later, Jesus Christ would be sold (betrayed) for the price of a slave—at that time, thirty pieces of silver.

V. Joseph's father, Jacob, was tricked with the blood of an animal into believing that his son was dead—just as Jacob had deceived his father, Isaac, with the skin of a dead animal.

VI. Pharaoh changed Joseph's name to Zaphenath-Paneah, which meant "the one who furnishes the sustenance of the land".

VII. The Nile River (called "Hapi" by the Egyptians) flows from south to north, emptying into the Mediterranean Sea. "Upper Egypt" is the southern portion, and "Lower Egypt" is the part of the land closest to the sea.

VIII. Egypt was divided into provinces called "nomes." Upper Egypt had twenty-two nomes, and Lower Egypt had sixteen. Each nome had its own capital and governor. Joseph's position placed him over *all* of these governors.

IX. Even though there were *eighty* gods and goddesses in Egypt, the earliest records written on tombstones of the old kingdom (2,680 B.C.) make reference to the "Great God" who judges the soul regarding immortality.

You feel certain that you would be wise to keep this scroll with you—you'll never remember everything. You tuck it into the waist of your kilt. You pick up the leather reins and hold them loosely in your hands. Your pulse quickens and excitement sends chills zinging through your fingers. You pull the smooth leather taut and suddenly....

(At the Beginning)

You find yourself on a grassy plain dotted with wild flowers. Wooded hills rise in the distance, and the sweet smell of clover is heavy in the sun-warmed air. The lazy drone of bees mixes with the calls of birds wheeling joyously in the deep-blue sky. Sheep graze all around you, their contented bleats soothing and restful.

A muffled groan of despair pierces the peace and you wheel around in the direction of the sound. You have never heard such agony in a voice before and your eyes search wildly for the source. Not far away, you notice a crumbling well—and the hollow groan seems to be coming from there. Several swift strides take you to the low wall, and you peer anxiously down inside. You notice absent-mindedly that no moss covers the stone walls—the well must have dried up long ago.

In the dark pool of shadows at the bottom of the pit, a young man crouches, his shoulders slumped in despair.

"Hey!" you call anxiously. "What are you doing down there?" You glance around, looking for a rope or a long, strong tree branch. "Wait a minute! There must be a way I can help you get out!"

An ashen face looks up at you. "Be careful, my friend," the boy calls urgently. "My brothers may throw you down here to die, too. Are they near?"

Nervously, you cast a hurried look over your shoulder. Several men cluster in the distance, gesturing to one another excitedly. Still farther away, a huge caravan is winding its slow way toward the

Decide Your Own Adventure 11

group of men. You turn back to the captive, uneasy.

"I think I see your brothers," you begin.

"Then hurry from this place!" he urges as the tiny flicker of hope in his eyes dies. "You must not try to rescue me—I would not have your blood on my head!"

"But I can't leave you here!" you protest, looking anxiously toward the men once more.

The young man's face relaxes into a sad smile. "I am not alone, my good friend," he says calmly. "If I die here, or if something else happens—I am in the Lord God's hands. Now hide yourself—for my brothers are in an ugly mood. Quickly!" he insists.

You scramble to your feet, alarm surging through your veins as you see that the caravan has joined the men and all are drawing much nearer now.

Your heart pounding, you break into a run for a cluster of trees. Ignoring the thorny branches that tear at your arms and legs, you crouch in a dense thicket of bushes.

"Here he is, Midianite!" a rough voice growls. "A fine specimen of healthy, young manhood to sell for a good price in Egypt!"

You carefully part the branches of a bush and peek out. You see ten Hebrew men of varying ages, all dressed in the distinctive, one-shouldered, multicolored tunics. Some of them are also wearing coats, as a protection against the sun. Fierce-looking men in turbans scowl down into the well, their golden earrings flashing in the sun.

"Pull him up!" one of the Midianites growls. "Let us see this 'fine, young specimen'!"

Joseph's brothers move away from the well, turning their backs on the two burly traders who haul Joseph up with a stout rope. *You should be too ashamed to watch!* you think angrily.

"For thirty shekels of silver, he is yours," says one of the Hebrew men.

"Thirty shekels! Do you think to rob us?" argues a Midianite. "He is not worth half that!"

You listen in growing horror as they haggle over the price for Joseph. Everyone shouts at once, arms waving in wild gesturing.

"Done!" barks the Midianite at last. "We'll pay you twenty shekels—but he'd better be as healthy as he appears!"

Joseph stands straight and unresisting as a leather collar is fastened tightly around his neck, a leash then tying him to the harness of a camel.

"Come!" growls a trader. "We have lingered here long enough." Heavily-laden camels, each tied to the camel behind, lumber past—and you see Joseph twist against his collar to cast one last look at his brothers and the land that has been his home.

The jingle of harness bells grows fainter as the caravan heads south. Sparing no looks for their brother, the Hebrew men head back to their flocks.

You have to decide what to do—should you follow the caravan? Perhaps you could learn from Joseph why his brothers hate him so. Or should you follow Joseph's brothers, and try to find the reason for their hatred from them. Either course could be dangerous. You think carefully, and then decide.

If you decide to follow the Midianite caravan, go to page 29.

If you decide to follow Joseph's brothers, go to page 34.

(You Have Decided to Go Backward In Time)

Dazzling white flames still leap and twist around the chariot. This has never happened before, you think uncomfortably. Your stomach knots as you find yourself wishing that you had chosen the course recommended by the steed.

The low voice chimes gently. "The Lord always leaves the choice up to us, little one. Often the right decision is the most painful."

"What happens now?" you question miserably. "Is the journey over?" You realize that you want more than anything to complete your quest—if only you could begin again!

The gentle sound of a thousand distant wind chimes splashes into the silence, and you realize that the steed is laughing softly. "No, little one, it is not over. You have far to go on this journey. I will take you back in time, to the beginning of the quest—and perhaps this time, you will make the right decision!"

Relief races like fire through your veins. You pick up the cool leather reins, and wait to begin again.

Go to page 11.

(You Have Come to the Birth of Benjamin)

You shiver as a wail of sorrow echoes eerily in the dusk. The setting sun bathes gentle hills in a blood-red glow, and one lone star wavers into life in the swiftly darkening sky above. Through the gathering shadows you see an old man stumbling toward you, leaving his large tent behind him.

"Rachel, Rachel . . . " he sobs quietly, as he throws himself to the ground beneath a low tree several feet away.

Pity washes over you as you realize that this must be Jacob, whom God named Israel. You remember that Rachel was his wife.

"Father!" calls a young man's voice urgently. Startled, you recognize Joseph running up the hill toward Jacob. He falters to a stop as he sees his father, and sharp alarm washes over his young face.

"You have a baby brother, Joseph," the old man says, his voice trembling. "We must give thanks to God for him."

Joseph sinks to his knees, putting his strong young arm around his father's shoulders. "Then why do you weep?" he asks anxiously. "They will not let me see mother — what's wrong?"

Jacob's shoulders heave. "Your mother is dead, Joseph. We must think of the child now."

Joseph's face is pale, and you see his lip tremble. "What is my brother's name?" he falters.

"Your mother named him 'Benoni, son of sorrow'," Jacob answers softly. "But I would not have him bear that name all his life. I shall call him

'Benjamin,' for he will be the 'son of my right hand'."

The father and son sit silently in the gathering dark, as the birds' sleepy twitters fade into the quiet of evening. Suddenly, the leaping flames of the chariot surround you, and you see the grieving figures no more.

"You have a question, my friend?" says the voice.

"Why weren't Jacob's other sons there to comfort him?" you ask. "Wasn't Rachel their mother, too?"

"No, little one. Rachel had only two children—Joseph and Benjamin. Remember that Rachel was Jacob's second wife, and the one that he truly loved. He was tricked into marrying Leah first."

The steed's voice continues quietly, "Do you know where you are?"

"No," you answer in bewilderment.

"You are in Bethlehem," answers the steed. "Here Benjamin, the son of my right hand,' was born.

"Now I may offer you two alternatives. You will go forward in time again. You may go to the time when Joseph's brothers are released from prison, or you may choose instead to visit a remote outpost of the Egyptian frontier, where soldiers are carrying out Joseph's instructions."

The voice falls silent, and you discover with a thrill that you would really like to see Egyptian soldiers at work—when will you ever again have such a chance? On the other hand, you'd like to see what happens after Joseph's ten brothers are released from prison. You take the reins in your hands, and pull them taut.

If you decide to see Joseph's brothers released from prison, go to page 108

If you decide to go to the Egyptian frontier, go to page 83.

Decide Your Own Adventure

(You Have Come to the Sheepfold)

Stars overhead sparkle in the rich velvet canopy of the night. The twinkling lights appear to have been flung by a great hand as though they were dazzling jewels to adorn the vast reaches of the heavens. Almost you can hear a faint echo of the symphony of creation, when all the morning stars sang together. In the distance, a stream flashes a silvery reflection of the rising moon.

As your eyes grow accustomed to the night, you see that you are halfway up a low mountain. Fir trees and boulders dot the slopes to the plain below, and the dark mouth of a cave yawns several feet away from you. Rosy flames suddenly burst into life on the plain below and in their glow you can see several men. Curious, you begin to pick your way through the piles of rock on the mountainside toward the campfire below.

Rowdy laughter shatters the contented peace of the night, and you hear the startled bleat of a sheep protesting. Around the fire, oblong circles of stones contain a layer of rushes—you think they might be beds. Over some of these rush cushions, the coats worn during the day as a protection from the sun have been spread to now serve as blankets. Crouching behind a large boulder, you look curiously at the men in the camp. Joseph's brothers half-sit, half-lie on their outdoor beds, laughing crazily. *They're drunk!* you realize in disgust.

You recognize a younger Joseph, his camel's hair cloak wrapped tightly about him, moving through the slumbering sheep. Stooping, he scoops a lamb gently into his arms and brings it toward the fire.

"This little one is badly scratched," he says softly, as he carefully pours a liquid from a ram's horn at his waist onto the wounded creature. The lamb bleats piteously once, then quiets under Joseph's gentle touch.

Your head jerks suddenly toward a movement in the underbrush—and you freeze in terror. The golden eyes of a lion glitter in the glow of the campfire! The beast stalks silently past you, its stare fixed on a sheep sleeping not six feet away. Crouching sphinx-like, the muscles in his powerful hindquarters ripple as he poises to spring. You stand frozen to the spot, unable to move or make a sound.

With a wild cry of "Lion!" Joseph leaps to his feet. In one fluid motion he throws his coat from his shoulders, scoops a heavy rod from its place by the fire and lunges toward the attacker.

The huge mouth of the beast opens in an ear-splitting bellow of fury. Teeth and claw flash as it springs in rage toward Joseph—then all is a confusion of fur and arms and furious sound. You grab a large, jagged rock, your heart pounding wildly. You glance quickly at the campfire, expecting to see Joseph's brothers rushing to his aid. Horror floods your limbs as you see them staggering in drunken confusion, stumbling over each other in an effort to rush away.

A raging roar is cut off abruptly and gurgles into silence. You turn back to see the lion fall into a limp heap. Frightened bleats of sheep echo across the

plain, as Joseph rises shakily to his feet, blood gushing from deep gashes in his arms. Standing over the dead beast, Joseph explains sadly, "The lone male, traveling without a pride, is a constant threat to our flocks—especially at night when the sleeping sheep are easy prey."

He wipes the sweat from his forehead with a forearm and peers anxiously into the night. "Grey-Ear!" he calls softly. A fat-tailed sheep fairly dances to Joseph's side. The boy's ashen face lights with delight as he kneels beside the sheep, flinging his wounded arms around it.

"That sheep came when you called!" you mumble in wonder.

Joseph turns toward you, a broad smile chasing away the lines of fatigue and fear. "Of course!" he answers happily. "All my sheep know my voice."

"Your brothers . . . " you falter, looking at their retreating figures in disgust.

"They were not much help," Joseph answers quietly.

"Well," you protest feebly, feeling faintly embarrassed for them, "maybe they thought it wouldn't matter, to lose just one lamb. After all, it *was* a lion!"

"*Every* lamb matters!" Joseph answers, frowning. "They know that—they are not hirelings, to run away from every danger. Our flocks are our lives; if we do not look after them, who will?"

A high, wavering bleat from near the campfire brings a gentle smile to Joseph's stern face. Swiftly he returns to the wounded lamb he had been tending, the larger sheep almost prancing behind him.

The night dissolves into the leaping, iridescent

flames of the chariot. You climb slowly in behind the steed, reflecting on the awesome bravery of the young Joseph.

"I am now allowed to take you several years into the future," chimes the musical voice, "to see Jacob send his sons to Egypt to buy grain. Or you may go a shorter time into the future, to see Joseph's brothers deceive their father into thinking that his son is dead. Which will you choose?"

You wonder which choice might help you more, and you reflect ruefully that nothing Joseph's brothers might do would surprise you after what you have seen this night! Unsure of which event to choose, you pick up the reins.

If you decide to see Jacob
send his sons to Egypt, go to page 93.

If you decide to see Jacob being deceived,
go to page 44.

24 Decide Your Own Adventure

(You Have Decided to Hear the Brothers' Plot)

You find yourself in a cluster of low trees. A clear, sparkling stream gurgles over shiny rocks and meanders through a narrow plain between densely-forested hills. Sheep and goats graze contentedly on the lush green grass, and the wide, startled eyes of a small deer peek briefly at you from the water's edge before the animal leaps swiftly away.

The sound of quarreling erupts from nearby and you peer through the trees in the direction of the voices. You instantly recognize Joseph's brothers, seated beneath a shady tree.

"Look!" shouts one, raising an arm to point into the distance. "Here he comes now—our brother, the dreamer!"

"Perhaps he is coming to rule over us now!" shouts another wrathfully. "Remember his heaven-sent dreams!"

Their bitter laughter makes you shiver—hatred is a tangible presence in this quiet grove.

Shading your eyes with your forearm, you squint into the distance. A solitary figure approaches, his long-sleeved robe swinging as his easy steed carries him across the plain. Even from here, you can see that the robe he is wearing is richly ornamented. Voluminous folds hang down to his ankles, and the bright colors swirl in the sunlight. Glancing back to Joseph's brothers, you see no coat to equal it; theirs are practical, durable coats of camel's hair or wool.

Decide Your Own Adventure

"Come!" The low voice, sharp with malice, sends chills up your spine. "Let us kill him and throw him into one of the pits!"

"A fine idea, Simeon!" laughs one. "But how do you suggest we explain his absence to our father?"

"We will say that a wild beast devoured him," comes the swift answer. "Then we shall see what becomes of his dreams!"

Dead silence follows, and you creep silently closer to the group. One look at their faces is enough to tell you that they are carefully considering the suggestion. You press your body against the rough tree bark, your heart hammering in dread, for you know that these men are in no mood to be overheard.

"No!" says a firm voice.

Startled, you jump nervously as an unfamiliar Hebrew man strides past you through the grove of trees. *Where did he come from?* you wonder.

"Reuben! You're the eldest!" protests one. "How can you have any love for that good-for-nothing? Just look at that coat he is wearing!"

"Well, what of it?" Reuben asks quietly.

"You know very well how our father feels about Joseph," his brother snaps. "The gift of that coat may mean that he has decided to give Joseph the double portion of goods that comes with the birthright—*your* birthright! Do you mean to tell me that you *want* to be ruled by that upstart?!"

Reuben's face is grave as he answers quietly, "You know well that I have no wish to be ruled by Joseph. But still— that is no reason to take his life!"

Reuben's nine brothers surround him. Their faces are murderously angry, and their eyes are hard with hate as they watch Joseph approach. Danger crackles in the air, and you wonder fleetingly if they are planning to kill Reuben, too.

"Shed no blood," says Reuben swiftly. "Throw him into the pit that is in the wilderness, but do not kill him. I must go now, to guard our flocks from the caravan that is coming this way." He looks anxiously at his brothers, but they have started toward Joseph, their faces hard and set.

He is planning to rescue him later, you think with relief. You know that he will not succeed, but at least he is not as heartless as his brothers.

The murderous faces of Joseph's brothers disappear in the shimmering fire of the chariot. Gratefully, you climb quickly inside, sickened by the hatred you have witnessed.

"Come." The steed's voice is clear and soothing. "I shall take you farther back in time now, to see Joseph guard his father's sheep. Mark well what you learn there."

This sounds relaxing, you think happily. *At least there shouldn't be any danger there!* You take the reins in your hands and wait.

Go to page 20.

(You Have Decided to Follow the Midianite Caravan)

The brambles tear mercilessly at you as you crawl out from your hiding place. Quickly you jog toward the retreating caravan making its way over the plain on a well-beaten path. Most of the traders have mounted donkeys and are far ahead—Joseph walks alone, tethered to the camel at his side.

"Why did your brothers do this to you?" you gasp as you reach his side.

Joseph's sorrowful eyes meet yours. "I knew they did not like me," he says softly, "but I never thought they would do this! They wanted to kill me!" he groans, "And they would have—but Judah suggested that they sell me instead!"

"Big deal!" you snort angrily. "He saved your life, and sells you into slavery?"

"No, no—you don't understand," Joseph protests, his face twisted in pain. "The others would have killed me, they were so filled with hatred. If Reuben had been here, he might have been able to talk them out of selling me, but as the eldest, it was his responsibility to guard the flocks. Many caravans pass through this plain, and they often help themselves to some of our animals. Reuben may have been planning to rescue me from the pit later, when tempers were cooler."

His eyes fill with tears and he looks fixedly ahead at the low mountains rising on the horizon. "My poor father," Joseph says softly. "This will give him such pain."

You look in disgust at the leather collar around

Decide Your Own Adventure 29

his neck. "Listen!" you say suddenly. "The traders will never see us—let me try to get this collar off of you!"

Joseph's eyes light in a smile, but he shakes his head gently. "No, my friend—but I thank you. Is not our God's name 'Yahweh Jireh,' meaning 'the Lord will provide'? I am in His hands, and I must submit myself to His will."

You stare at him in amazement. He has been betrayed by his brothers, who wished to kill him. The degrading collar of slavery chafes his neck as he is led against his will away from everything and everyone he has ever loved—and yet he is confident that the Lord will provide! *How could anyone hate this man?* you wonder miserably.

"But *why*?" The question bursts from your very soul. "Why do they hate you so much?"

Joseph's gaze is faraway. "Well, you see," he begins softly, "My father and I have... *had* a special relationship. I have always loved to hear about God, and His dealings with our family. I never grew tired of hearing how my father, Jacob, wrestled with an angel of the Lord!" he continues, his eyes sparkling with excitement. "Or how the Lord God provided the sacrifice when my grandfather Isaac went up the mountain with his father, Abraham. But my brothers," Joseph pauses, his brow wrinkling into a frown of bewilderment, "had other interests. They thought that our father loved me best—as if he gave so much love to me that there wasn't any left over for them!"

You reflect for a moment. "But that's stupid!" you begin slowly. "Love isn't like an apple, so that

when you give some away there is less for everybody else! Surely your father loved them too."

Joseph nods vigorously. "Of course he did—but I think that sometimes they did not want to believe that. And when they did things that I knew the Lord God would not like, I told our father," he finishes simply.

You feel a little uncomfortable at this. *He tattled on his brothers,* you think—*no wonder they grew to dislike Joseph!* "You mean," you ask stiffly, "if they made a little mistake, you told your father?"

Decide Your Own Adventure 31

Joseph's eyes widen in astonishment. "Of course not!" he protests. "That would be foolish tale-bearing, and would lead only to strife. No, I told our father only about the things they did that would make the Lord God angry! I wish, though," he says slowly, "that I had not told my brothers about the dreams."

"What dreams?" you ask curiously, moving hastily away from the camel, which is eyeing you with a nasty look.

Joseph's lips curve into a grin, and you remember suddenly that he is, after all, still a teenager.

"No, they were not happy about the dreams!" he laughs softly. "Perhaps I *was* showing off just a little. But I was curious to see what my brothers thought the meaning could be."

"What did you dream?" you inquire.

"Well," Joseph begins slowly, "In the first dream, my brothers and I were binding sheaves in the field. Suddenly my sheaf rose up and stood erect, and their sheaves gathered around and bowed to my sheaf." A sparkle of mischief flashes in his eyes, as he continues, "In my second dream, the sun and the moon and eleven stars were bowing down to me." Joseph's face clouds, remembering. "Even my father rebuked me when I told him—I think perhaps I should have kept the dreams to myself."

A sudden pain in your foot stops you in your tracks. You sit hastily upon a boulder, digging in your sandal for the sharp rock that has lodged there. Suddenly the entire landscape is blotted from sight by dancing, iridescent flames—and you see the chariot waiting silently. You climb thoughtfully aboard behind the steed, wondering what will happen next.

A voice—seeming to come from the milky-white steed itself—chimes musically. "Now you must make a decision," says the voice softly. "You may decide to go back in time, to see Joseph guard his father's sheep—or you may go back to hear Joseph's brothers plot against him. Which will you choose?"

You already like Joseph, and would welcome talking with him at a time before the terrible event of today. Your blood runs cold at the idea of an encounter with his brothers, but you think carefully about which choice might prove to be more helpful on your quest, then take the reins in your hands. You make your decision, then pull the reins taut.

If you decide to go back to the sheepfold, go to page 20.

If you decide to hear the brothers' plot, go to page 25.

Decide Your Own Adventure 33

(You Have Decided to Follow Joseph's Brothers)

You jump as a huge hand clamps forcefully on your upper arm, pulling you out from your hiding place. Thorny branches tear painfully at your arms and you look up into the scowling face of a Hebrew.

"What are you doing here?" he roars, "Do you think to spy on us?" His red face is inches from yours, and his eyes glitter angrily.

"No, no —" you stammer uneasily, "I wasn't spying. I just wondered why your brother was in the well."

His eyes narrow dangerously. "You know that good-for-nothing is my brother, do you?" he growls menacingly. "Perhaps you know more than is good for you, dog!"

34 Decide Your Own Adventure

Mercilessly he propels you ahead. "How do you come to be here?" he questions harshly. "I don't remember seeing your ugly face before. Do you belong to the traders?" His strong hands spin you around to face him.

Your mind races for an answer—for you dare not tell him you are from a country he has never heard of, and a time far into the future! Pain shoots down your arms as his grip on your shoulders tightens.

"Are you deaf, boy?" he bellows. "Answer me!" He deals you a resounding slap against your ear, making your head throb and your ear ring.

Other Hebrew men cluster around him, eyeing you with suspicion and distrust. One of the men steps forward, his face creased with worry.

"That's enough, Simeon. Let him alone!" he says

Decide Your Own Adventure 35

quietly. Then, hurrying over to the well, he peers anxiously into the shadows. "The boy is not here!" He throws his head back and utters a piercing shriek of grief, his strong hands rending his tunic. "What am I to do?" he wails, his face contorted with agony.

The brothers mutter uneasily, forgetting you for the moment. You ease quietly out of the center of the group, watching carefully.

"You planned to rescue Joseph, didn't you, Reuben?" accuses Simeon in a furious hiss.

With tears tracing paths down his dusty cheeks, Reuben stares in bewilderment. "Yes, of course," he answers as he walks slowly toward his brothers. "I assumed you would all come to your senses."

Simeon's lip curls in disgust; he turns his back on Reuben and speaks to the others. "Here is what we must do," he says briskly. "We must slaughter a goat and dip our brother's fine new tunic in the blood. Then we will bring it to our father to examine for himself. It is the only way," he adds, shrugging carelessly.

"What about him?" asks one, pointing angrily toward you. "He has seen everything—he could ruin us all!"

Your throat suddenly dry, you try not to tremble as they all glare at you in fury.

Reuben speaks, quietly and compellingly. "Shed no blood, my brothers—do not touch the stranger. Have you not done enough evil this day?" Reuben pulls you toward him, his grip strong on your shoulders. "You *will* keep silent, will you not?" he half demands, half questions.

You nod vigorously, knowing that you dare not tell anyone what you have seen because you are not allowed to attempt to change history in any way. "I *must* keep silent," you answer honestly.

A brief smile flits across Reuben's face. "He will not speak," he says convincingly. "Come. We must return to our father. He must be concerned about us, or he would not have sent Joseph." Anguish twists his face once more, and you see him struggle with emotion. "We have many miles to go—let's be off."

Decide Your Own Adventure 37

Dancing white flames suddenly blot the scene from view and your heart leaps with delight to see the chariot of fire standing silently before you. A low voice, sounding almost like the pure chimes of bells, seems to come from the beautiful white steed.

"It is time for you to leave this place," says the voice quietly.

You scramble quickly into the chariot, grateful to be taken away.

"I am allowed to take you several years into the future, when Jacob sends his sons to Egypt to buy grain. Or you may go several days into the future, to see Joseph's brothers deceive their father into thinking that his son is dead. Which will you choose?" The bell-like voice falls silent.

You think carefully about which choice might help you more on your quest. Taking the smooth leather reins in your hands, you pull the reins taut and make your decision.

If you decide to see Jacob send his sons to Egypt, go to page 93.

If you decide to see Jacob being deceived, go to page 44.

(You Have Decided to Go to the Slave Market)

You squint in the brilliant sunshine reflected off the dazzling white stone buildings. Monkeys chatter and crowds of Egyptians shout in excitement as they barter with merchants. You look in amazement at the variety of goods being traded: graceful ivory cups, golden platters, spices, white linen woven so finely it is almost transparent, huge piles of fruits and vegetables, and even monkeys are being traded in this jostling, cheerful marketplace.

"Slave for sale!" shouts a voice. You whirl around to find yourself staring into the glittering, dark eyes of a Midianite trader. His turbaned head and flashing golden earring seem familiar to you, and you cast a swift glance behind him for Joseph.

A proud, slender youth stands quietly—you recognize Joseph immediately. His calm, grey eyes are focused on a point faraway, his neck is raw and bleeding where the leather collar has rubbed against it during the long journey. The Midianite gives the leash a sudden cruel jerk, and tears of pain spring to Joseph's eyes.

"Step forward, dog!" growls the Midianite. "You had better pray that you bring more than twenty shekels—I'll kill you before I feed you any longer."

Several Egyptians crowd around Joseph, eyeing him curiously. A short, thick-set man prods Joseph's arms.

The Midianite's lips curve into a rusty smile. "You'll not find fat on this one's bones, my good

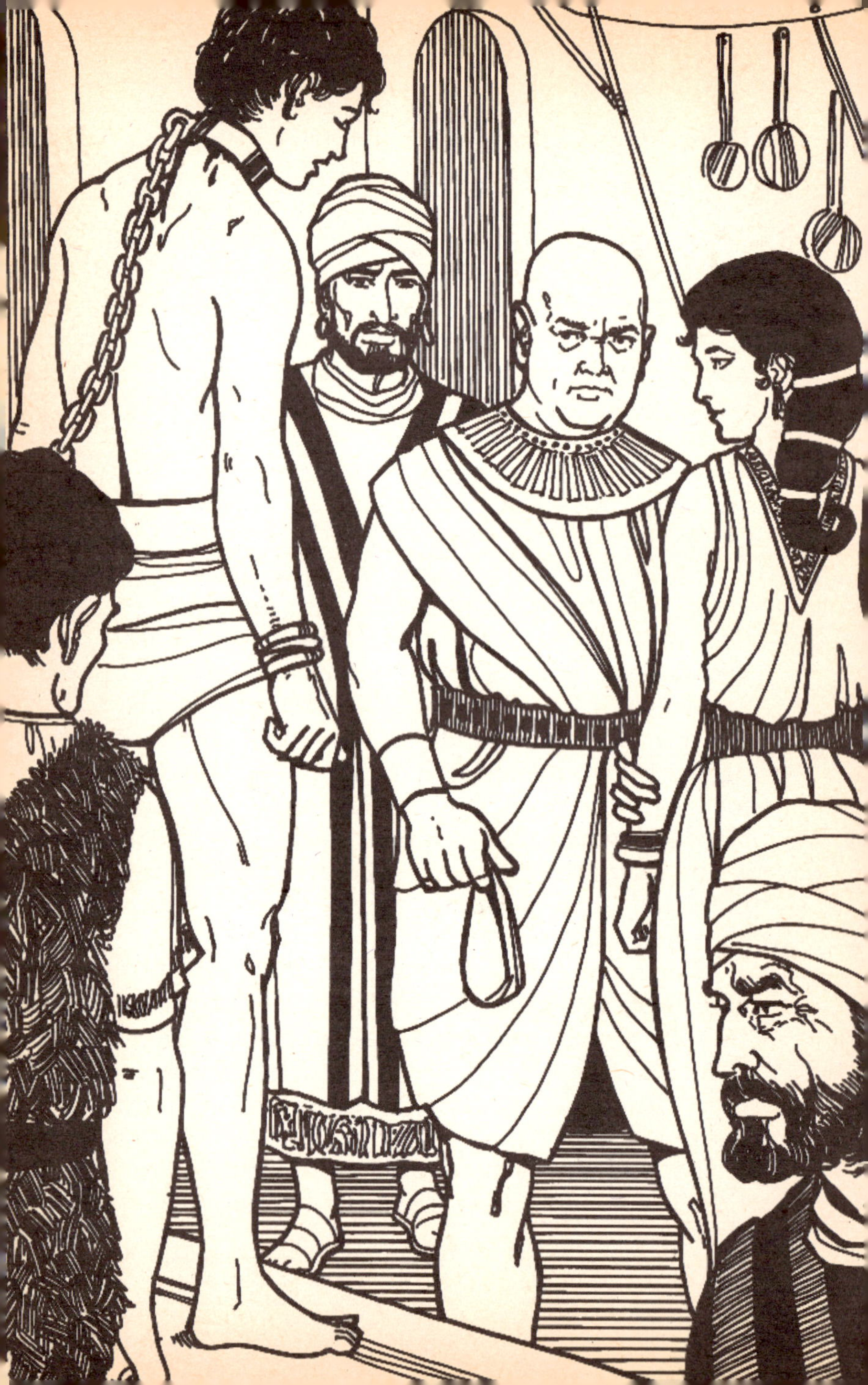

man. He is young and lean, and ready to give you years of service—and at such a low price!"

"Are you going to buy that one, Potiphar?" calls a woman's voice.

The Egyptian pulls Joseph's lips roughly back from his teeth, peering into his mouth. "Healthy teeth," he mutters. "He looks strong enough. What price?" he asks the Midianite abruptly.

His eyes narrowing greedily, the Midianite whines, "It will break my heart to part with him, master—but I can let you have him for forty shekels of silver."

"Forty shekels!" the Egyptian shrieks. "Do you think I am an idiot? I'll not pay more than twenty! Look—do you see any muscles in this arm?" he demands, pinching Joseph's arm.

Your heart aches for Joseph's humiliation, and you wonder how he can stand the terrible grief. The Egyptian pokes and pinches him as if he were an animal.

"I like this one, Potiphar. Settle on a price, and let's go home," purrs a woman's voice just behind you.

You turn to see a young and very beautiful woman eyeing Joseph wickedly. As the stocky Egyptian man turns toward her with an adoring smile, the sultry look in her eyes is swiftly replaced with one of innocence. She gazes up at her husband and coos, "He looks as if he would be a very good slave for you, my dear husband."

"Do you think so, my pretty?" the man says with a foolish, smitten look on his face.

"I wish for my husband to have nothing but the *very* best," she whispers.

Decide Your Own Adventure 41

The Egyptian grins happily. "Very well, wife." He turns to the Midianite, "But twenty shekels is my top price—take it or leave it!" he says firmly.

The woman smirks happily as Potiphar counts the silver coins into the trader's hands. Your skin crawls with revulsion as you see her run a caressing hand down Joseph's arm. His face reddens uncomfortably as their eyes meet—and the woman's invitation is unmistakable.

Potiphar turns to Joseph, swiftly removing the leather collar from his neck. "I'm sure I'll not need this," he says, not unkindly. "Work hard, and do well—and you will find me a good master. You shall have the good fortune to work in the pharaoh's own household, since I am the captain of the guard! Come now," he says abruptly, "You will begin to learn your duties today!"

Joseph falls obediently into step behind Potiphar, and they wend their way through the crowd. Dancing white flames blot them from view, and you sink back gratefully into the chariot of fire. Your heart is heavy with grief for this young man who has done nothing to merit his brothers' wicked hatred and betrayal. With a shock, you realize, *this is one way that Joseph was like a foreshadow of Christ—he was hated for no reason by his own people!*

The quiet voice of the steed answers your unspoken thoughts. "Yes, little one," murmurs the voice, "You are right.

"Now you must make a choice. You may go forward in time, to see the wickedness of Potiphar's wife..."

"No! Please!" you interrupt, shuddering at the

thought. You feel that you have already seen enough of the spoiled, childish woman. *How could I possible learn anything that would help me on my quest by seeing Potiphar's wife one more time?* you wonder. What is my other choice? you ask.

You may go back in time," answers the steed, "but I would recommend the first choice."

Perhaps I could learn from the past why Joseph is sometimes called the foreshadow of the Savior, you think. Or should you make the choice that the steed recommends, even though you hate the thought? You take the reins in your hands, and decide hastily.

If you decide to see Potiphar's wife, go to page 52.

If you decide to go backward in time, go to page 16.

Decide Your Own Adventure

(You Have Decided to See Jacob Being Deceived)

You find yourself standing beneath a grove of trees. Before you, neat squares of beans alternate with plots of melons, their vines twisting snake-like over rich black earth. Terraces of gnarled grape vines carpet the low hills, and bees buzz beneath fig trees laden with fruit. An old man, his eyes shaded with his forearm, stands peering anxiously into the distance.

Your stomach twists uneasily as you see Joseph's brothers slowly approaching their father, their weary donkeys plodding between the fields. You see the old man's face, puzzled and anxious, as he searches the group in vain for his beloved Joseph. At last, the brothers halt before their father, and dismount. You see that their tunics are torn in the age-old symbol of mourning, and your heart skips a beat. Jacob's face crumples in fear.

"We found this," says one of the men, thrusting the richly-ornamented folds of a robe toward Jacob. "Please examine it to see whether it is your son's or not."

No one notices you walk quietly toward the group. You see that the crumpled robe is horribly blood-stained. Jacob shakes out the folds with trembling hands; huge gashes in the blood-soaked fabric draw a vivid picture of mutilation and ghastly death. Your heart aches for Jacob, as he clutches the robe to his heart with a broken sob of inconsolable grief.

"It is my son's tunic," he gasps. "A wild beast

Decide Your Own Adventure   45

has devoured him! Joseph has surely been torn to pieces!" The old man's knees buckle, and he sinks to the ground; he lifts his face toward Heaven and groans as if his very heart is torn apart.

Tears sting your eyes at the awful sight of this old father's terrible grief, and you turn away. You remember fleetingly that Jacob himself deceived his own father with the skin of a slain animal—now his sons deceive him by almost the same means. Jacob's desolate wail pierces you to the heart, and your tear-blinded eyes almost fail to notice that the shimmering flames have mercifully hidden the awful sight.

"Be comforted," soothes the low voice of the steed. "He will see his son again. Now you must make a decision. I am allowed to take you to a slave market in Egypt, where you may see Joseph sold. Or you may go to the household of Potiphar, where Joseph labors."

You remember that you must find out how Joseph was like Daniel, and why Joseph is sometimes called the foreshadow of the Savior. Which choice might help you more? You think carefully, and make your decision.

If you decide to go to the slave market, go to page 39.

If you decide to go to Potiphar's house, go to page 47.

(You Have Decided to Go to Potiphar's House)

A light breeze fans your cheeks softly as you stand on the banks of the Nile. Rosy fingers of the setting sun touch the water with flame, and a bird flutters suddenly from the thicket of reeds at your side. A light skiff floats down the river, close to the bank where you are standing.

"Just one more, Potiphar. Please?" begs the lovely young woman in the skiff.

Her muscular companion gazes at her adoringly. "Very well, my lovely wife—but only one. Not even for you will I stay on this river once the sun has set!"

You watch them curiously as they both peer intently into the reeds. Potiphar half-crouches forward, his stocky form powerful and alert. In one hand he grasps a thick, carved stick. Suddenly, the young woman's lips part in an eager, excited cry—she claps her hands sharply, and a bird flies up from the reeds. In one fluid motion, the stick leaves Potiphar's hand, and the fowl falls dead into the water.

"Your aim is sure, my husband," coos the woman. "You!" she snaps, pointing right at you. "Fetch my husband's throwing stick!"

You wade into the water, and grasp the floating stick. Glad you can swim, you head for the skiff.

"Stupid!" the young woman shouts. "Bring the fowl also!"

Grimly, you retrieve the dead fowl, and bring both to the light boat. Potiphar smiles pleasantly at you, and you can see that he is much older than his wife—and more kind as well! Her eyes sweep indifferently over you as you wade through chest-deep water back to the bank.

A man stands silently on the bank. With a start, you recognize Joseph. He is several years older, and his powerful frame is that of a mature man—but his face is still kind. He stretches a friendly hand toward you, pulling you from the water.

"Joseph!" shrills the woman's voice. "Why are you here? You should be attending to the details for our banquet!"

"Now, my lovely," rumbles Potiphar's calm voice. "You know well that everything under Joseph's hand prospers. Do not crease that beautiful forehead of yours. Come! We shall go home and ready ourselves."

The skiff moves out of sight, and Joseph smiles pleasantly. "I see that Potiphar's lovely wife required your services," he chuckles, looking at your drenched tunic.

48   Decide Your Own Adventure

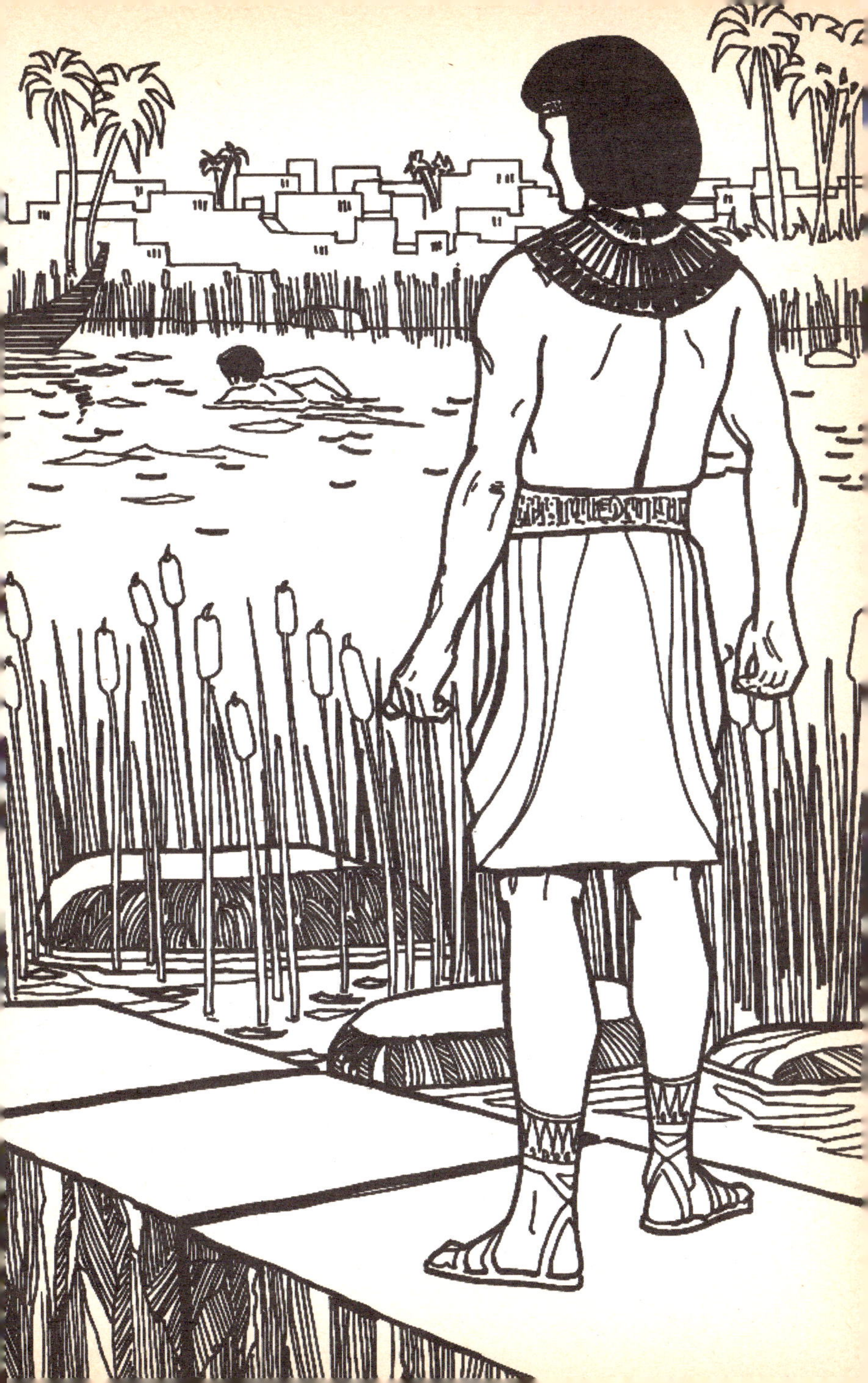

"I don't think she is lovely," you grumble. "I think she is rude!"

Joseph laughs softly. "Getting our own way all the time often makes us rude, my friend. She is to be pitied, you know."

"Pitied!" you cry, astonished. "Why?"

Joseph puts a friendly arm around your shoulders as you walk away from the river. "It is no kindness to spoil anyone. When her beauty fades, she will lack the true beauty that comes from within. Her husband will grow tired of her cruel ways when the bloom of her youth has fled—and she will wonder why she is old, and unloved," he sighs.

You shiver suddenly in the dusk, for the air has grown sharply cooler. A slender obelisk towers into the gloom, its sides covered with carved figures and hieroglyphics. A flash of light from its top startles you, and you gasp, "Where is that light coming from?"

Joseph's voice is calm and steady as he answers, "Simply the metal crown on top of the obelisk catching the last light, my friend."

"Why is it covered with a metal crown?" you puzzle.

Joseph sighs. "The purpose of the obelisk is to glorify the sun, which the Egyptians worship as a god. They cover the top with metal to reflect the sun's glory."

The two of you walk silently toward a huge, walled enclosure just ahead. Joseph gives you a friendly pat as you reach the gate.

"Here I must say good-by," he smiles. "My master is giving a very special banquet tonight, and I must be sure that all is in readiness. By the grace of God, I will see you again!" He waves briefly, and turns into the courtyard.

Radiance floods the eerie stillness of the Egyptian night, and you climb happily into the chariot of fire. The steed's voice is welcome.

"You may now go forward in time," says the voice, "to see the wickedness of Potiphar's wife, or you may go backward in time. I would recommend the first choice," the steed adds gently.

You shudder at the thought of Potiphar's wife, for you do not like her already. Should you make the choice that the steed recommends, even though you hate the thought? Or should you try to by-pass this choice and go back in time, instead? You take the reins in your hands, and decide quickly.

If you decide to see Potiphar's wife, go to page 52.

If you decide to go backward in time, go to page 16.

(You Have Decided to See Potiphar's Wife)

You find yourself in a large, high-ceilinged room. Two narrow beds, slanting gently down at the foot, tell you that this must be a bedroom. Potiphar's wife, her fingers laced behind Joseph's neck, does not even notice you pressed against the wall in the shadows.

"You are so handsome," she coos, her hands caressing Joseph's shoulders. "Potiphar is middle-aged and fat!" she pouts, her ruby-red lips moving closer to Joseph's. "He is no fit husband for a young woman. But you...."

Joseph is miserably uncomfortable. "My lady," he says gently, "I am certain that you would not wish to betray a husband who loves his wife as dearly as Potiphar loves you."

The young woman steps back in anger. "I care *nothing* for him, do you hear?" she insists. I *shudder* when he touches me! My beauty is *wasted* on Potiphar! But surely," she whispers, moving closer to Joseph, "my beauty moves you?"

Joseph eyes her sternly. "Your husband has been good to me, my lady. He has put all that he owns in my charge and has trusted me completely. He has withheld nothing from me except you, because you are his wife. Now do you ask me to betray his trust with this great evil?"

"Oh, Joseph," she moans, winding her arms around his neck, her lips inches from his own. "Lie with me — Potiphar need never know! It can be our secret, yours and mine." The young woman pulls

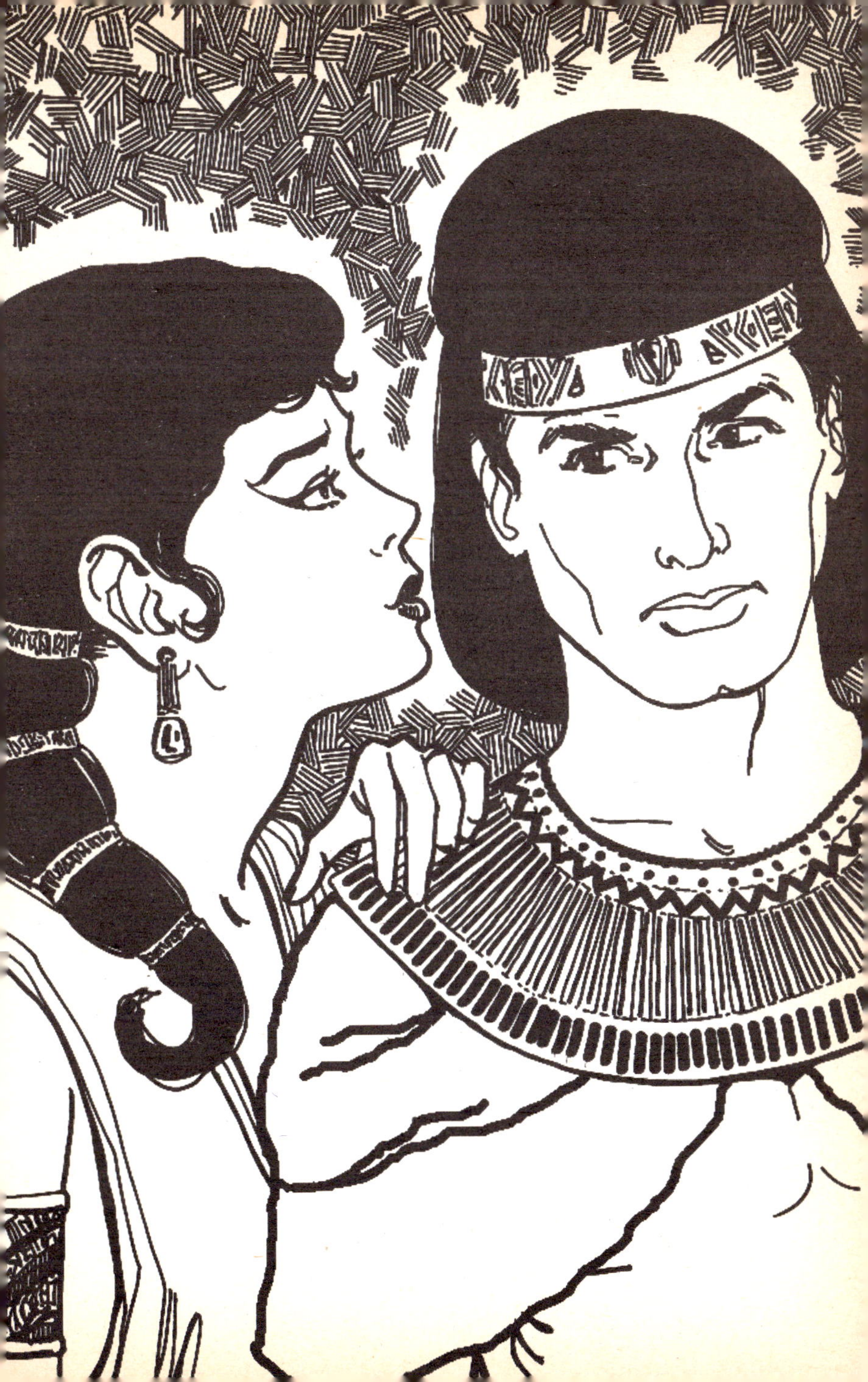

on Joseph's garment, tugging urgently.

"How could I do this great evil, and sin against God?" Joseph explodes, his face flushed and angry. He pushes her away firmly, but the temptress has her hands entwined in his tunic.

"Joseph!" she begins, her eyes flashing dangerously, but Joseph twists away—his tunic slips from his shoulders and he pulls his arms from it in order to escape her grasp. He runs from the room, his face filled with anger and revulsion.

Squirming miserably, you flatten yourself against the wall. You watch the young woman pace like a caged lion. Then suddenly, she looks at the tunic lying on the floor and smiles wickedly. She flings herself on the bed and claps her hands. A manservant hurries into the room.

Potiphar's wife raises a trembling hand, tears flowing from her dark, liquid eyes. She is the very picture of a pathetic child as she quivers, "Joseph came into my room to lie with me!" she accuses, and the servant's eyes grow wide. "I screamed! And when he heard me raise my voice, he fled, leaving his garment here beside me!" One slender hand points, trembling, to Joseph's tunic on the floor beside her.

You burn to shout the truth as the servant's shocked gaze rests on the tunic—but you know you may not alter history in any way. Potiphar's wife collapses into a delicate heap, her shoulders shaking gently as she sobs. Your heart begins to hammer as Potiphar himself enters the room.

Swift strides take him to his wife's prostrate form. "What is wrong, my lovely?" he murmurs.

"What has happened to upset you?" He lifts her to a sitting position, one arm encircling her in a protective manner.

She shudders, then rests her head on her husband's shoulder. "The Hebrew slave, whom you brought to us, came in to... to have his way with me!"

Potiphar gasps, then draws back from his wife with a frown. "Are you talking about *Joseph*?" he asks incredulously.

The young woman trembles, her slender hands whisking Joseph's tunic into view. "I raised my voice and screamed, Potiphar," she cries, "and he dropped his garment in his haste to flee. This is what your slave did to me!"

Potiphar's eyes are locked onto Joseph's tunic

and only you can see the flash of triumph in his wife's eyes as she hands the tunic to him. With a roar, he leaps to his feet. His face is flushed with rage and his eyes burn. "I have entrusted *everything* to him—and he has repaid me with treachery! Now he shall pay for *this* crime!" he rages.

Potiphar storms out of the room bellowing, "Bring Joseph to me!" His wife follows swiftly, eager to see Joseph punished because he has humiliated her.

To your relief, the glowing steed appears. You climb quickly into the chariot, feeling angry and frustrated.

The steed speaks quietly as the flames enfold you. "You are upset, my friend?"

"Yes!" you explode angrily. "Joseph was unjustly accused! It's not fair!" Suddenly, a blinding realization flashes through your mind. *Jesus Christ was unjustly accused! Here is another way that Joseph was like Christ!*

"Yes, little one," answers the steed gently. "You are learning.

"But now you must make a decision. You may go ahead in time to see Joseph in jail, or you may see the Pharaoh's butler and baker in jail the morning after their dreams."

Thoughtfully you make your decision.

If you decide to see the butler and baker, go to page 61.

If you decide to see Joseph in prison, go to page 57.

(You Have Decided to See Joseph In Prison)

You find yourself in inky darkness, and shudder as an insect scuttles lightly across your bare legs. Stretching out your arms, your hands find rough, stone walls. You are straining to see in the darkness when the sound of breathing nearby sends chills up your spine. You bite your lips in horror, for you could never have imagined how awful it would be to sit in the black depths of a dungeon—forgotten and afraid. A slit of light suddenly appears on the floor several yards away, and your heart beats faster.

Light from a torch floods through the opening doorway into the room. You squint painfully, your eyes hurt by the sudden light after the total darkness.

"Joseph, my friend!" a man's voice shouts. "You came back!"

"Of course I came back, old friend!" the man in the doorway laughs gently. "Am I not also a prisoner?"

As your eyes grow accustomed to the light, you see that the dungeon is a vast, bare room. Counting swiftly, you find that there are twenty men here, their faces lit with joy as they look at Joseph fondly.

"Now, let's have some light in this hole," says Joseph cheerfully, setting the torch he carries into an empty niche in the wall. The flame dances cheerfully, chasing away the gloom.

"Why did you come back, Joseph?" asks a tired-looking middle-aged man, his forehead wrinkling into a frown. "You could have escaped!"

Joseph smiles slightly. "How could I betray the

Decide Your Own Adventure 57

trust of the chief jailer?" he asks quietly. "He has put me in charge of everything down here. I could not run away!"

"*I* could!" snaps a young man. "In fact, what's to stop me from knocking you out and escaping right now?"

Murmurs of agreement rumble in several throats, and your scalp prickles. *How could Joseph stop these men? Only he stands between them and escape!*

Joseph's face is calm and untroubled as he answers, "There is nothing to stop you, my friend. I must trust you, as the chief jailer trusts me."

You steal a glance at the men sitting on the filthy dungeon floor. Each struggles with conflicting emotions; the desire to be free, consideration of Joseph's words, shame, despair, resignation. Finally, the man nearest you speaks.

"Well, Hebrew, I guess you can trust us. Perhaps

Decide Your Own Adventure 59

we should all learn more about this God of yours; He hasn't gotten you out of this prison, but He surely seems to prosper everything you touch!"

Joseph smiles, his face glowing. "I will gladly teach you about the God of Abraham, Isaac, and Jacob. And while we speak," he adds with a twinkle in his eyes, "we can make this dungeon fit for humans again!" He steps outside the door, and carries back two heavy wooden buckets, water sloshing over their sides.

The men shout happily, and one cries, "Soap and water! Thanks be to your God, Joseph! I am weary of living like an animal in a cave!"

Joseph grins. "We shall be clean and well-fed, my friends. I will take the best possible care of us!"

Brushes and brooms heaped outside the prison door soon are in each man's hands, and they are so busy working that they do not see the glow of the chariot of fire in the corridor outside. You walk thoughtfully toward your steed, and climb in behind him.

"I shall take you forward in time now," says the voice. "It is time for you to learn what happens the morning after the butler and baker have their dreams."

You remember that the butler, or cupbearer, and the baker are prisoners with Joseph—and that he interprets their dreams. Eagerly, you take the reins in your hands.

Go to page 61.

(You Have Come to See the Butler and the Baker)

The vibrant crow of a cock startles you as you squint into the ruddy glare of the rising sun. The air smells fresh and clean, and early morning dew drenches the hardpacked earth of the courtyard. You are standing in a huge, walled courtyard. Large rooms built against the walls bustle with hushed activity. The clean, elegant lines of a two-story mansion set in the center of the courtyard throw sharp shadows on the western ground.

A tall, well-muscled man strides from one of the rooms, carrying a huge tray. With a jolt, you recognize Joseph—older, but still with the same kind face. You hurry behind him in the early morning stillness as he turns down narrow stone steps in the far corner of the courtyard. You descend into gloom, the guttering torches on the wall making the shadows leap and dance eerily.

At the bottom of the steps, two corridors stretch into the distance." At the end of one, you see Joseph placing his tray on the floor. From a huge key ring that hangs from his waist, he selects a key, fitting it into the lock on a massive wooden door. Picking up his burden once again, he pushes the door open with his foot, and enters. You hurry down the corridor, and peer cautiously through the open doorway.

At the far end of the vast, empty room two Egyptians sit on the floor. Their shoulders are slumped wearily, and their faces are drawn and sad. No sunshine will ever find its way into this underground

Decide Your Own Adventure

cavern of a room—it would be pitch black if it were not for the single torch set in the wall.

"Good morning, my friends," says Joseph pleasantly as he sets his tray down on the floor in front of the men. "I was able to bring your favorite fruit, baker. Look!" he smiles, as he points to an earthen bowl heaped with slices of melon.

One of the men casts Joseph a despairing glance, then buries his face in his hands.

"Why are your faces so sad today?" Joseph asks gently.

"We have each had a dream," moans one, "and there is no one to interpret it."

You remember that dreams were very important in ancient times, and that interpreting them correctly was considered vital.

"Do not interpretations belong to God?" asks Joseph softly. "Tell it to me, please. Perhaps I may be His messenger."

The older of the two sighs with faint hope. "In my dream," he begins, fixing his eyes earnestly on Joseph's face, "behold, there was a vine in front of me; and on the vine were three branches. And as it was budding, blossoms came out, and produced clusters of ripe grapes."

Joseph watches the man intently, his face concerned.

"Now Pharaoh's cup was in my hand," the man continues, "so I took the grapes and squeezed them into Pharaoh's cup, and I put the cup into Pharaoh's hand." His voice falters to a stop, as he watches Joseph.

Joseph smiles at the cupbearer. "I will tell you

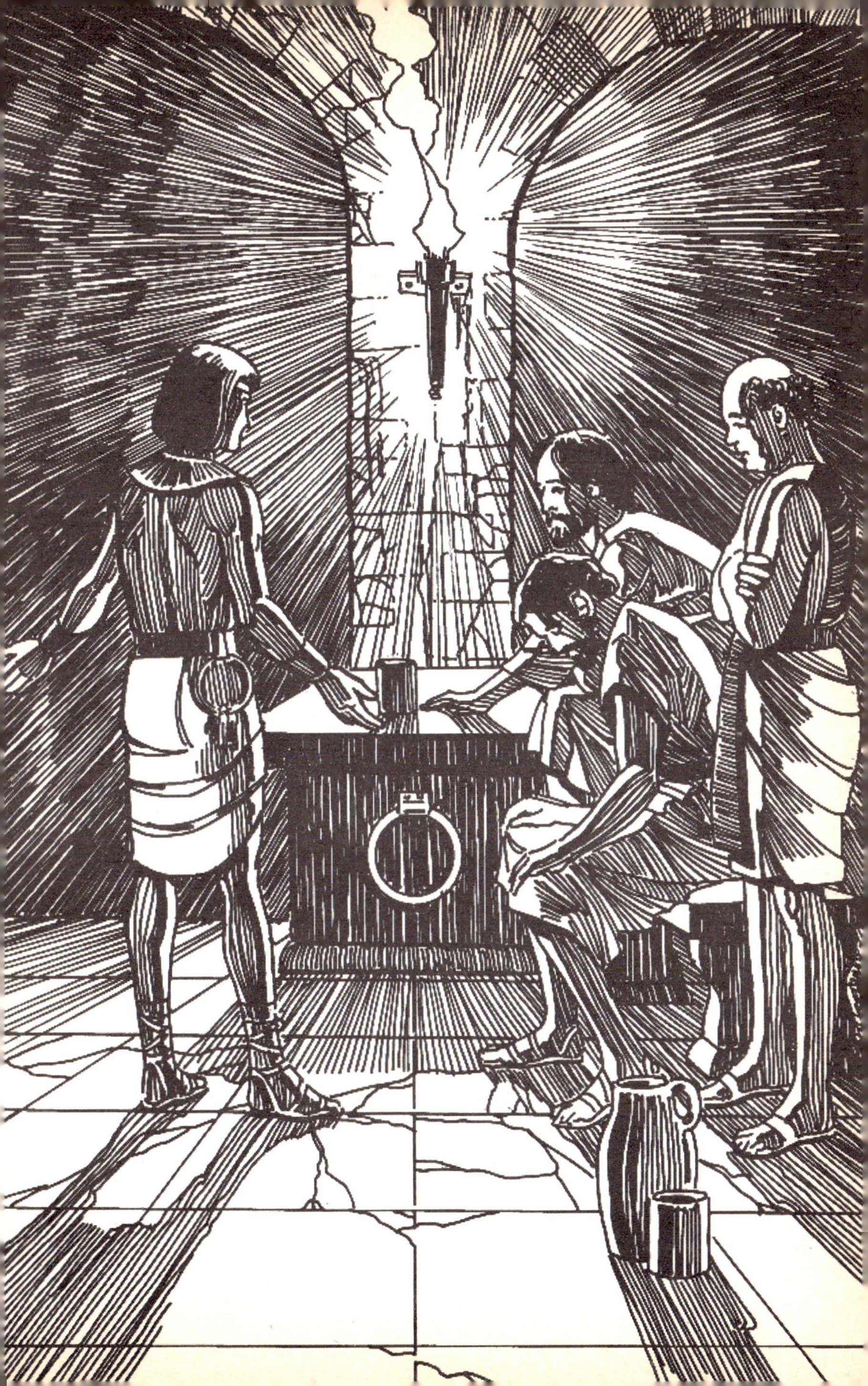

the interpretation of your dream," he answers. "The three branches are three days; within three more days Pharaoh will forgive you and restore you to your office; and you will put Pharaoh's cup into his hand according to your former custom when you were his cupbearer."

The man's eyes are wide with astonishment and hope; his delighted shout echoes in the dungeon. Joseph's face grows grave, and he places his hands on the cupbearer's shoulders.

"Only keep me in mind when it goes well with you," he requests, "and do me the kindness of mentioning me to Pharaoh, so that I might get out of this prison. For I was in fact kidnapped from the land of the Hebrews, and even here I have done nothing that they should have put me into the dungeon."

The cupbearer nods happily in agreement, and the baker—seeing some hope for himself—suddenly grasps Joseph's wrist.

"I also saw in my dream," the baker begins, "and behold, there were three baskets of white bread on my head; and in the top basket there were some of all sorts of baked food for Pharaoh, and the birds were eating them out of the basket on my head."

Joseph's eyes grow dark with compassion, and he kneels beside the baker. The man's face contorts with fear in the silence, and his anguish grows deeper when Joseph rises and places a comforting arm around his shoulders.

"This is its interpretation," begins Joseph, great sadness in his gentle voice. "The three baskets are three days; within three more days Pharaoh will lift up your head from you and will hang you on a tree; and the birds will eat your flesh off you."

A heart-rending wail of grief bursts from the baker's throat. The cupbearer looks on in horror as Joseph speaks low in the stricken man's ear. A brilliant glow throbs in the corridor behind you, and you step into the chariot of fire gladly.

"Were the interpretations right?" you whisper as the flames hide the dungeon from your sight.

"Yes, little one," answers the steed.

"And did the cupbearer mention Joseph to Pharaoh, as he promised?" you ask anxiously.

"No, he forgot Joseph the moment he was let out of prison," answers the voice. "For two more years Joseph will stay imprisoned in this place."

"But, wait a minute," you begin slowly. "Joseph doesn't *seem* to be imprisoned. After all, he had keys to the dungeon—he even brought the prisoners their breakfast!"

"He is truly imprisoned, my friend," says the steed softly. "But the Lord blessed Joseph, and the chief jailer favored him; Joseph was put in charge of all the prisoners in the jail."

"If he was in charge," you falter, "then he wasn't under lock and key. So why didn't he escape?"

The steed's bell-like laughter chimes softly. "Joseph delighted in doing the Lord's will, my friend. He knew that if the Lord God wished for him to be in charge of the prison, that that was what he must do. Do you understand?"

It must have taken a lot of faith and courage to trust in the Lord so completely, you think in awe.

"Now it is time for your decision," says the voice

Decide Your Own Adventure

briskly. "I am allowed to take you more than two years into the future, to the time of Pharaoh's troubling dream. You may go to the temple of the magicians, or to the court of Pharaoh himself. Decide quickly, friend."

A thrill of excitement makes you tingle, as you make your decision.

If you decide to go to the temple of the magicians, go to page 67.

If you decide to go to Pharaoh's court, go to page 71.

(You Have Decided to Go to the Temple of the Magicians)

Thick patches of fog curl snake-like around two sloping sandstone pillars on either side of you. The pillars are tall pyramids, and as you gaze up toward the tops, you see that they are cut straight across, instead of being pointed. An eerie pre-dawn stillness makes you shiver as you watch wisps of grey mist curl around the bases of the pillars. The sound of bare feet slapping across a polished stone floor makes you whirl around to peer inside the temple.

A priest hurries between the soaring pillars of the court, his lips moving soundlessly. He beckons you to follow, and you stride after him— breaking into a trot as he disappears into a room at the side of what must be the main temple.

You burst into the room to see the priest muttering anxiously as he fumbles through rolls of papyrus. Amazed, you see shelf after shelf crammed with all sizes of tight rolls.

"Here, take these," he says shortly, thrusting several rolls toward you.

You scramble to take them without dropping any, as the priest plops into a low chair. His shoulders slump in fatigue as he lowers his shaven head into his hands.

"What shall I do?" he moans. "I cannot find the meaning of Pharaoh's dream anywhere! What answer am I to give him?"

You shift uneasily from one foot to the other, the stiff parchment rolls jabbing painfully into your bare arms.

Decide Your Own Adventure

"Ah!" the priest cries suddenly. "I have one course left open to me. Put those down, and follow me!" he snaps, as he leaps to his feet.

You trot swiftly after him as he hurries into the next room. A polished wooden table in the center of the room is cluttered with papyri, as well as vials of different colored liquids. Motioning curtly for you to stand at the side of the table, the priest carefully pours water from a delicate ivory jug into a engraved silver goblet. His lips move soundlessly as he lifts his gaze heavenward.

Abruptly, his arm sweeps a clear space on the table; papyri and vials clatter to the floor. The priest removes the stopper from one of the remaining vials, and tips the contents slowly into the goblet. Reverently, his face frowning in concentration, he places the goblet upon the table. The priest peers intently into the goblet, his lips slightly parted. You stand frozen to the spot, sensing that you dare not interrupt.

"Bah!" he snarls as he straightens. "Nothing! The gods refuse to grant me the interpretation! Divination by the cup has never failed me before!"

"How are you supposed to find the meaning of the pharaoh's dream?" you question hesitantly.

The priest glances at you impatiently. "In the dream manuals, of course. Only no dream like this has ever been recorded—so of course the dream manuals cannot tell me what happens to those who dream that particular dream!"

"Dream manuals?" you ask timidly.

"Yes, yes. Don't you know anything? Throughout history, scribes have recorded strange dreams.

Then they record what happens afterward to those people who *had* the dream. In this way, we know what a particular dream means."

You frown in bewilderment. "But what difference does it make, whether you know the meaning of a dream or not?"

The priest's eyes widen, and he stares at you curiously. "The gods send dreams, youngster. How do we know what they are telling us, if we do not understand the meaning? But enough of this chatter," he says firmly. "I must go now to Pharaoh's court, where I will inform him that all my arts cannot give me the meaning of his dream." His lips tighten in irritation. "We shall see if the Hebrew prisoner can do any better at interpretation than I have done!"

The Hebrew prisoner! you think in excitement, *That can only be Joseph!* Hurrying after the priest, you jog out of the temple into the courtyard. Grey mists flee as the blazing flat disc of the sun erupts over the eastern horizon. Huge statues of Egyptian gods line the wide stone-paved streets, and you have a blurred impression of vast marble columns as you enter the cool shadows of a huge building. Winding through polished halls, you find yourself at last in a crowded throne room. You squeeze in behind a delicately-carved column and take stock of your surroundings.

The chatter of many different languages ebbs and flows through the hall like a tide. Between the shoulders of people from many lands, you see the pharaoh himself seated on a polished throne. A disturbance at the rear attracts your attention, and you crane your neck to see what is happening. *This is going to be interesting!* you decide joyfully.

Go to page 75.

70   Decide Your Own Adventure

(You Have Come to Pharaoh's Court)

Carved stone pillars soar ceilingward to end in delicate lotus blossoms. The cool marble floor is polished to a high gloss. On a dais at the far end of the room, the imposing figure of the pharaoh paces furiously from one side to the other. A broad, jewel-encrusted collar spills richly down his chest, and the golden threads in his cloth headdress sparkle.

Magicians cluster uneasily, their shaven heads glistening with nervous sweat. You peer through the crowd, and with a start you recognize the older Egyptian man you had last seen in prison. His brow is furrowed in thought, as he watches the angry pharaoh pace.

Hesitantly, the older Egyptian speaks. "I would make mention today of my own offenses," his says slowly, his deep voice mournful.

The pharaoh's steps halt, and he wheels around to confront the older man. "Well, cupbearer!" he snaps irritably. "Tell me your offenses!"

"Pharaoh was furious with his servants, and he put me in confinement in the house of the captain of the bodyguard, both me and the chief baker," the Egyptian says, his voice growing stronger as he continues. Pharaoh watches him intently, and you realize that the cupbearer, above all others, would have Pharaoh's trust—for only the cupbearer would stand between the pharaoh and death by poison!

"And we had a dream on the same night, he and I," he says, his gaze faraway as he remembers. The

Decide Your Own Adventure

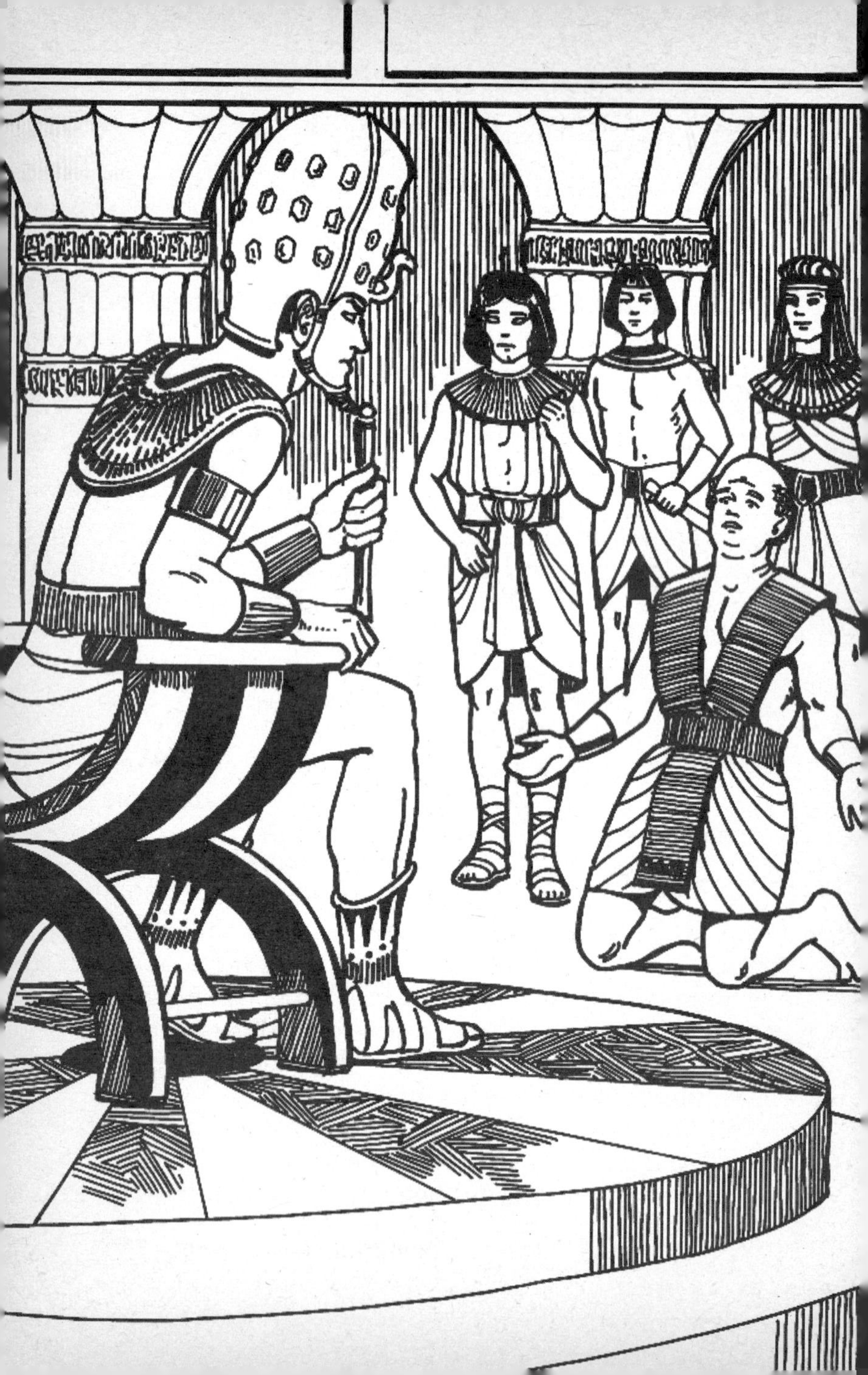

magician beside you draws his breath inward in a sharp hiss; everyone in the room is paying close attention now.

"Now a Hebrew youth was with us there," the man continues, "a servant of the captain of the bodyguard, and we related our dreams to him, and he interpreted our dreams for us."

A spark of hope leaps into Pharaoh's dark eyes, and he sits heavily on the bejeweled throne, never taking his eyes off the cupbearer's face.

"And it came about that just as he interpreted for us, so it happened," says the Egyptian wonderingly.

An electric silence crackles in the room; the priests' faces are a mixture of annoyance and relief. At last, the pharaoh claps his hands sharply.

"Have the youth brought to me at once!" he commands. The room leaps into activity, as servants

Decide Your Own Adventure

hurry out. The priests murmur quietly, huddling in groups. The cupbearer looks steadily at Pharaoh.

"This will take a little time, my Pharaoh," he says calmly. "The prisoner must be shaved, and must be dressed in garments fitting for a royal audience."

"I care not how much time," says Pharaoh heavily, "But I *must* know the interpretation of my dream, for my spirit has troubled me."

Like a thunderbolt, you are jolted by the memory of another king who was troubled in spirit because he did not understand the meaning of a dream! Nebuchadnezzar was the king, and Daniel the prophet who interpreted the dream—*so this is how Joseph is like Daniel,* you think in delight. *Joseph and Daniel were both prisoners in a strange land, and both were given the interpretations of a king's dreams by God!* You slip behind a massive pillar, joyous that you have accomplished at least the first part of your quest. You cast a swift glance around for the chariot, relieved that you see no sign of it for now—for you'd like to see Joseph again. You lean gratefully against the cool stone, thinking that you won't have too long to wait!

Go to page 75.

74   Decide Your Own Adventure

(Joseph and Pharaoh)

Hushed excitement ripples through the crowd as Joseph walks confidently into the throne room. He wears the simple, white, knee-length kilt of the Egyptian, but even with no jewelry he somehow manages to look kingly as he approaches the pharaoh. His newly-shaven face glows with health, and he halts at the foot of the dais, looking Pharaoh directly in the eye.

"I have had a dream," the pharaoh begins abruptly, "but no one can interpret it. I have heard it said about you, that when you hear a dream you can interpret it."

Joseph's untroubled gaze falls on the cupbearer, who hangs his head guiltily. *He should feel guilty,* you think resentfully; *he forgot all about his promise to mention Joseph to the Pharaoh until two years later!*

"It is not in me;" Joseph replies quietly. "God is the one who will give Pharaoh the understanding he seeks."

Pharaoh frowns, darting an doubtful look at Joseph from beneath lowered brows. The room is so still that even a breath would seem loud.

"In my dream, behold, I was standing on the bank of the Nile;" says Pharaoh slowly. "And behold, seven cows, fat and sleek, came up out of the Nile; and they grazed in the marsh grass." Bewilderment is clearly stamped on his face as he continues, "And lo, seven other cows came up after them, poor and very ugly and gaunt, such as I had never seen for ugliness in all the land of Egypt; and

Decide Your Own Adventure 75

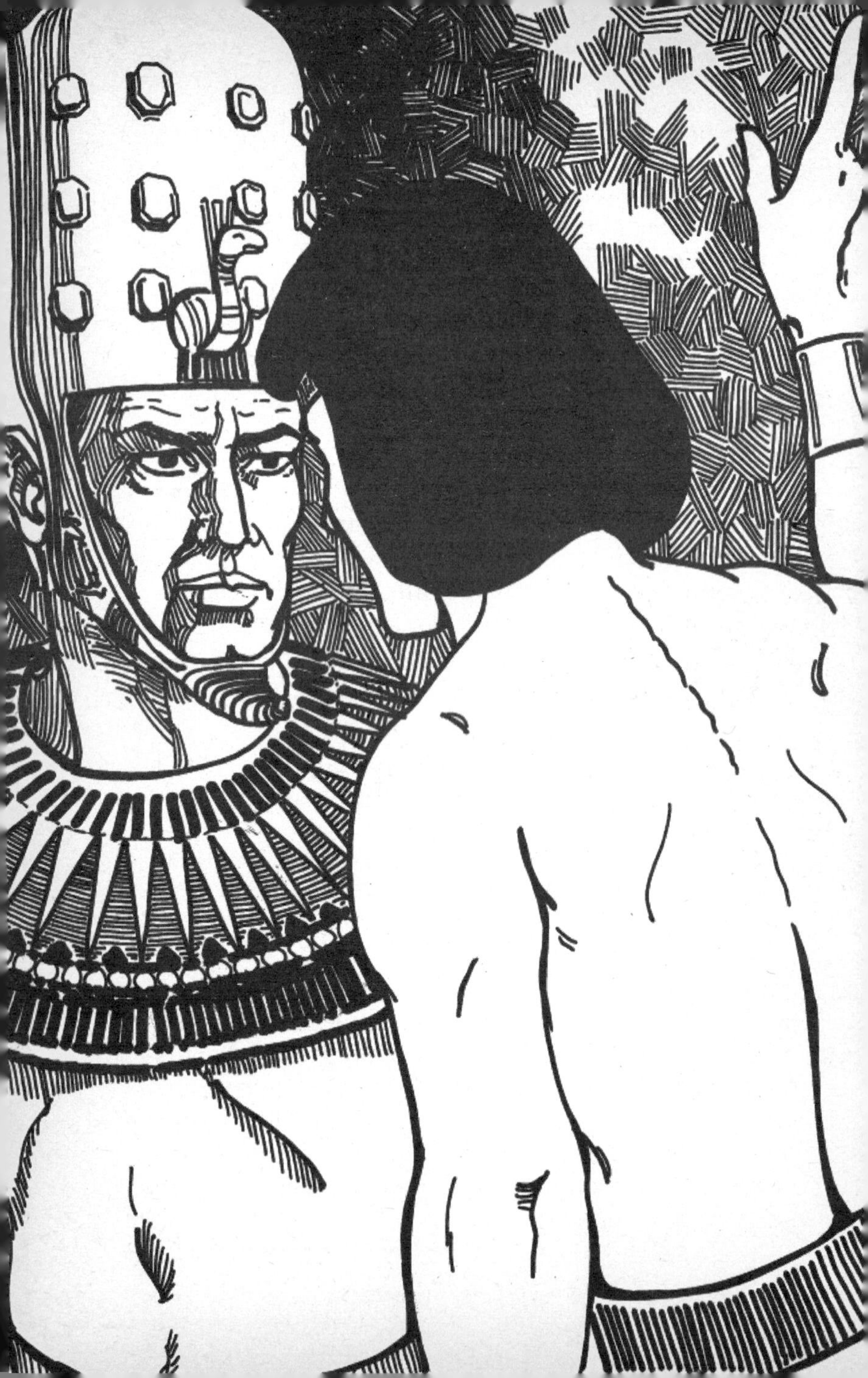

the lean and ugly cows ate up the first seven fat cows!"

Joseph stands quietly, and Pharaoh continues, almost scowling. "Yet, when the lean cows had devoured the fat cows, it could not be detected, for they were just as ugly and lean as before. Then I awoke."

Still Joseph says nothing, and the entire audience seems to hold its breath. Pharaoh continues, his voice low with dread. "I saw also in my dream, and behold, seven ears, full and good, came up on a single stalk; and lo, seven more ears, withered, thin, and scorched by the east wind, sprouted up after them; and the thin ears swallowed the seven good ears." Pharaoh's face has drained of color, and his eyes are troubled. "Then I told it to the magicians, but there was no one who could explain it to me," he finishes, fixing an anxious gaze on Joseph's face.

Joseph smiles comfortingly, and the pharaoh sinks back in his jeweled throne, watching him intently. "Pharaoh's dreams are one and the same;" Joseph begins confidently. "God has told to Pharaoh what He is about to do."

You glance quickly at the sea of faces in the throne room; the priests are especially eager to hear what Joseph has to say.

"The seven good cows are seven years, and the seven good ears are seven years; the dreams are one and the same."

"But what do the years mean?" you hear a priest whisper urgently.

"The good cows and good ears mean that there

Decide Your Own Adventure

will be seven years of abundant harvest. And the seven lean and ugly cows that came up after them and the seven thin ears scorched by the east wind represent seven years of famine."

A gasp erupts from the crowd, and you realize that in these times a famine that lasts for seven years could mean death for thousands of people.

Joseph continues calmly, his untroubled voice falling like soothing cool water on the anxious audience. "It is as I have spoken to Pharaoh: God has shown to Pharaoh what He is about to do. Behold," Joseph's voice grows in strength, "seven years of great abundance are coming in all the land of Egypt; and after them seven years of famine will come, and all the abundance will be forgotten in the land of Egypt; and the famine will ravage the land."

A stricken, haunted look of pain springs to the pharaoh's eyes; you wonder if he has seen the results of so severe a famine before, and you suddenly pity him.

"Now as for the repeating of the dream to Pharaoh twice," continues Joseph, "it means that the matter has been firmly decided by God, and God will quickly bring it about."

Pharaoh's shoulders slump in despair as he buries his head in his hands. A low wail, quickly stifled, sends chills up your spine. The cupbearer's troubled eyes fill slowly with tears as he watches Joseph.

Joseph's voice is gentle as he continues, "And now let Pharaoh look for a man discerning and wise, and set him over the land of Egypt. Let

Pharaoh take action to appoint overseers in charge of the land, and let him save a fifth of the produce of the land of Egypt in the seven years of abundance."

Pharaoh's head snaps upright, hope sparking in his dark eyes.

"Let the overseers gather all the food of these good years that are coming, and store up the grain for food in the cities under Pharaoh's authority, and let them guard it," continues Joseph. "And let the food become as a reserve for the land for the seven years of famine which will occur in the land of Egypt, so that the people may not perish during the famine."

A chorus of excited shouts burst from people in every corner of the room. A slow smile begins in the Pharaoh's eyes, then spreads to his face as he looks at Joseph. Pharaoh looks with affection at the excited crowd of his advisors. "Can we find a man like this, in whom is a divine spirit?" he says, grinning at the crowd's enthusiastic roar.

"Joseph! Joseph!" the crowd chants happily.

Pharaoh steps down from the dais and places his arms upon Joseph's shoulders. "Since your God has informed you of all this," he says quietly, "there is no one as discerning and wise as you are. *You* shall be over my house, and according to your command *all* my people shall obey you; only with respect to the throne will I be greater than you."

Startled, you realize that Pharaoh believes Joseph completely—and you wonder if it might be possible that God has put His truth into the heart of an Egyptian king!

The crowd cheers wildly as Pharaoh slowly pulls a heavy gold ring from his finger and slides it onto Joseph's. "Bow the knee!" a voice rings out, and to a man, every Egyptian in the room sinks to one knee.

Pharaoh's voice rises strongly. "Though I am pharaoh, yet without your permission no one shall raise his hand or foot in all the land of Egypt," he pronounces solemnly.

The jubilant crowd squeezes in to congratulate Joseph and out of the corner of your eye you catch sight of the familiar glow of the chariot in the dim hallway behind you. No one notices you slip

80   Decide Your Own Adventure

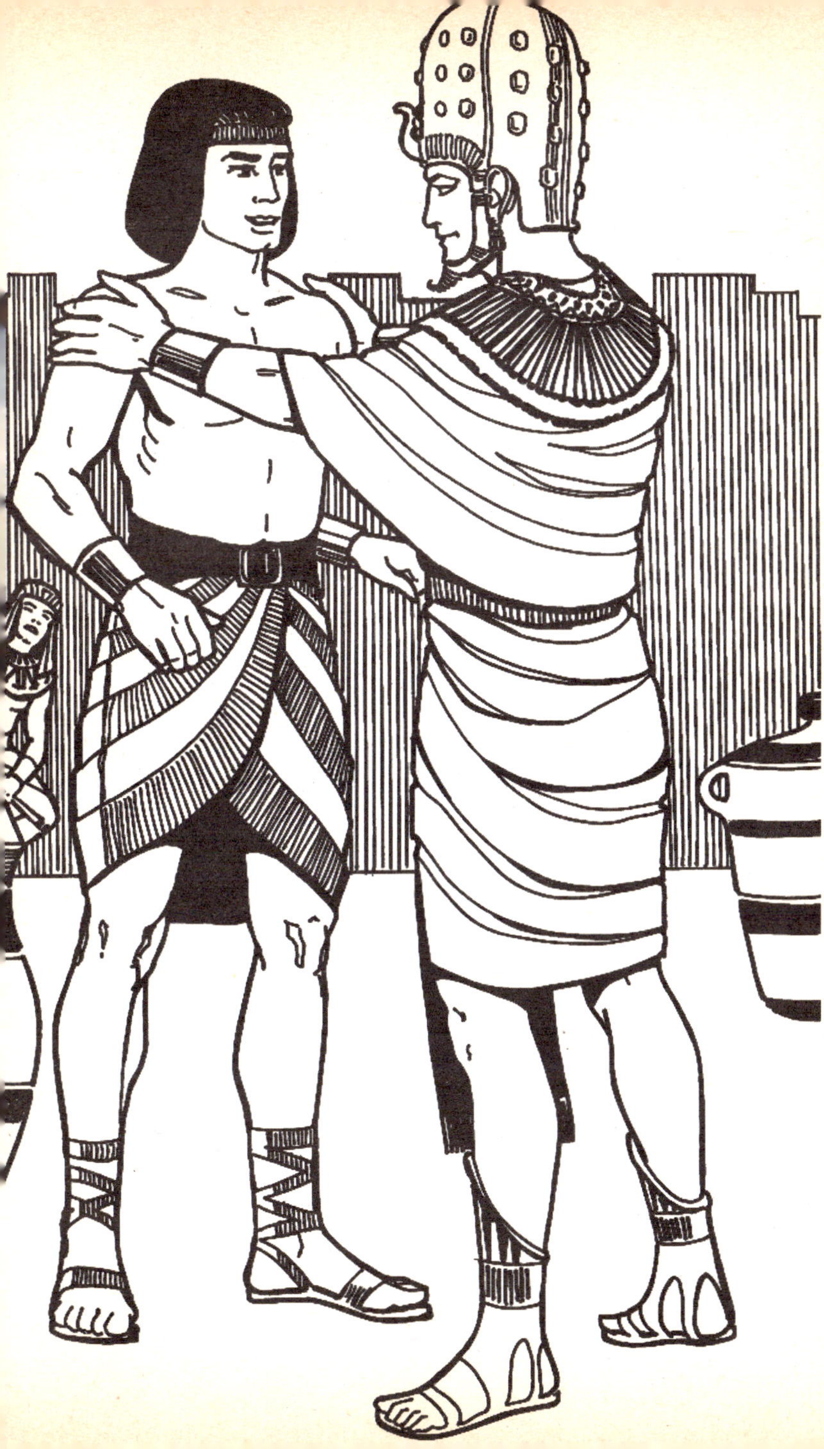

quietly out of the throne room to climb in behind the beautiful steed.

"Pharaoh made Joseph ruler over all Egypt," you say in amazement, "second only to himself! I guess I never realized how powerful Joseph really was!"

The steed's musical laughter echoes softly. "He was indeed powerful, little one. But now you must jump more than seven years into the future. You may decide to see Joseph's brothers in Pharaoh's court, or you may join them in prison. Which will you choose?"

You realize that you would really like to see Joseph's brothers bow before him—thereby fulfilling the dream that made them so angry many years before! On the other hand, would it be more helpful to your quest to join his brothers in prison? You think carefully, and make your decision.

If you decide to join Joseph's brothers in prison, go to page 105.

If you decide to see Joseph's brothers in Pharaoh's court, go to page 100.

(You Have Decided to Go to the Egyptian Frontier)

The thunder of horses' hooves pounding the dusty earth startles you, and your heart leaps into your throat as you see a chariot bearing down on you. You dive swiftly out of its path, and a confused blur of sweaty horses streaks past. As the dust settles, you peer after them, shading your eyes with your forearm in the blazing desert sun.

Rising from the foot of rocky cliffs, a solid fort stands menacing and alone. A quick look down the road in the opposite direction reveals no more chariots, so you strike off in the direction of the fort. After a few minutes of walking, you reach your destination—and stand staring up at the sturdy gates.

A sudden, sharp pain in your back precedes the snarling command, "Halt! State your business or die!"

Thoughts tumble through your brain, as fear seizes you by the throat. "I am here for Zaphenath-Paneah," you stammer, as you cautiously turn around.

The scowling face of a soldier confronts you, his spear aiming now at your heart. Suddenly his face relaxes into a grin. "Ha!" he roars gleefully. "And *I* am here at the express wish of Pharaoh himself! You'll have to come up with a better excuse than that, youngster!" he laughs. "But I think you're harmless enough. What are you doing here?"

"I wanted to see the fort," you answer simply. The soldier lowers his spear, chuckling softly.

Decide Your Own Adventure

"Now *that* has the ring of truth, at least! Well, you'd better follow me into the fort," he says, propelling you briskly along beside him. "We're expecting an attack on our supplies by the Nubians any time now—and you'll be safer inside. Come along!"

You hurry beside him into the massive stone fort—noticing as you go through the gates that the walls are at least twenty-three feet thick! Jogging across the courtyard, you follow the soldier up brick stairs, and into a cool, dim hallway buzzing with activity.

Light filters through slits in the walls, and an archer stands at each slit—his bow at the ready. Other soldiers carrying spears hurry through the hall toward yet another stairway, more narrow than the one you have just used. Your escort turns to you with a friendly smile, beckoning you to follow.

"You may come up to the turret, youngster," he says softly, "but you may only stay for a moment, mind you."

You follow quickly up the narrow steps, puzzling over an unfamiliar sound that grows louder all the time. Emerging into blinding sunlight, you squint painfully into a blazing blue Egyptian sky. Crossing the turret, you lean your arms on the stone parapet and gasp at the scene below.

The Nile river roars and rages over the boulders in its way. *So this is the sound I heard,* you reflect, as you resist the impulse to clap your hands over your ears. Across the river another fort perches on rocky cliffs, and you see the sun glinting off spears in the turrets opposite.

Your companion grins. "We're in a pretty good

position to protect our storehouses here," he says with a chuckle. "Although *I* don't see any sign of a drought, myself."

An older soldier, his face leathery, frowns forebodingly. "Zaphenath-Paneah hears the voice of God, you foolish boy," he snaps. "If God says there will be a drought, there will be! But Egypt will not go hungry."

A younger soldier sneers, contempt gleeming in his eyes. "We all know how you feel, Mersu. But perhaps you've soldiered in the sun too long! We have never known such plentiful harvests — guarding these stores of food is a waste of time, believe me."

"You'll sing a different tune when the seven years of drought begin," says the soldier angrily. When all the world comes to Egypt to buy grain, you'll bend your knee in thanks to the God of Zaphenath-Paneah."

Several soldiers chuckle good-naturedly, as Mersu squares his shoulders defiantly. Your companion turns to you with a laugh. "All right, youngster!" he says, "Now be off with you. You've seen your fort!"

You're heading down the narrow steps, when the flames surround you.

"Now you will go forward in time," say the steed. "Joseph's brothers returned to Canaan with the grain they bought from him—but the grain ran out, and still the famine continued. They have returned to Egypt, to buy more—only *this* time, they have brought Benjamin with them. So here is your choice," chimes the voice. "You may join Joseph's brothers as they speak with his steward, or you may see the banquet which Joseph has prepared for them."

You think carefully, then make your decision.

If you decide to see Joseph's brothers speak to the steward, go to page 118.

If you decide to see Joseph's banquet, go to page 120.

(You Have Decided to Join Joseph on the Nile)

You find yourself on the bank of a river—*the Nile!* you think in excitement. High overhead, the blazing disc of the sun hangs in a deep blue sky. Palm trees sway in the hot desert breeze, and huge pyramids jut into the sky in the distance. You wheel around as a whir of wings flashes from a dense clump of papyrus reeds a few feet away; a ragged-crested kingfisher hovers oddly over the sparkling river. Intrigued by the dense thicket of reeds, you make your way to the edge, parting the stalks to peer into the thicket. The reeds suddenly wave violently, as something large lunges through them. Your heart leaps into your throat as you see a crocodile moving swiftly toward you through the stalks.

Searching frantically around, you see no safety on the bank and without thinking, you plunge into the river. Swallowing a huge gulp of water, you begin to swim desperately through the warm water—heading for the middle of the river. You risk a hasty glance over your shoulder and see the log-like form of the crocodile gaining on you; terror makes your flailing arms weak.

A high-prowed boat, its sail taut with captured wind, bears down upon you. "Help!" you yell desperately, forcing your aching arms and legs to move still faster.

The high prow looms overhead, and suddenly your world is a chaotic whirl of water and shouts and deathly fear. You have sunk beneath the

Decide Your Own Adventure

surface, and as you stare up through the green water, you glimpse yellowed rows of enormous teeth just inches away. A strong hand grasps you firmly under the chin, pulling your head out from underwater. Another hand grabs the back of your shirt and, choking and gasping for breath, you feel yourself pulled up past the side of the boat. You collapse on the deck. Through the roaring in your ears, you hear excited shouts turn to laughter.

"You got him! That crocodile won't bother us further!"

You raise yourself shakily on one elbow, wiping the water from your eyes.

"You were blessed, my friend," says a quiet voice

behind you. "That crocodile wasn't really hungry, or you would not be here now!"

The kohl-lined, grey eyes of your rescuer regard you calmly. "Here," he says kindly, lifting you to your feet. "You need to recover a bit."

With a jolt, you recognize Joseph—thirteen years older now. Your knees still wobbly, you follow him into the shade of the boat's cabin, which appears to be leather stretched over a wooden framework. Joseph guides you gently into a low, carved chair and settles himself comfortably on a facing chair.

"Now, youngster," he says, his eyes twinkling, "how came you to be racing a crocodile today?"

Your fear melts as you look into his kind face. "You saved my life," you gasp.

His face crinkles into a merry smile. "Oh, that was indeed my pleasure! I do not approve of crocodiles having youngsters for supper."

Joseph claps his hands sharply twice and a servant bows almost instantly in the arch of the cabin door. "I think we will have some light refreshment now, if you please," he says pleasantly.

"As you wish, Zaphenath-Paneah," says the servant, bowing low.

Remembering that Joseph has been a slave for these past thirteen years, you marvel at the position of authority he now seems to hold, and that you sense no hint of bitterness or self-pity in his character. "What am I to call you, please?" you stammer.

Joseph's eyes dance. "I think I would prefer you to call me by my Hebrew name, Joseph," he says with a chuckle. "The Egyptian name fairly breaks my jaw!"

The smooth motion of a ship under sail ceases abruptly; the boat begins to surge forward in rhythmic bursts accompanied by the sound of many oars dipping in and out of the water. Cautiously, you rise from your low chair to stand at the cabin door. The oarsmen's shoulders glisten with sweat as they propel the craft toward the nearby bank. You glance behind you to see another boat following closely, also making for land.

After a few short moments, the mooring stake is pounded securely into the bank. Several servants scramble off the other boat, hurrying toward Joseph's.

"Is that your boat too?" you ask curiously.

Joseph nods. "Yes, of course. When my duties

call for me to travel, my kitchen boat must follow. I trust," he adds with a smile, "that your adventure has left you hungry!"

Suddenly aware that you are ravenous, you scramble hastily back to your chair. A bowing servant places a huge, golden platter piled high with fruits before Joseph, while another follows with a basket of flat breads. An older servant places a large, empty bowl between you and Joseph. You watch carefully as your host holds his hands over the bowl while the servant pours water over them, then offers a snowy white rectangle of linen as a towel. You quickly do the same and, with a bow, the servant removes the bowl.

You look to Joseph to see what the next step will be and see him spread his hands out over the meal. "Blessed art Thou, Jehovah our God, King of the world, who causes bread to come forth from the earth," he says softly. "Now, my friend," he addresses you with a smile, "please share my meal."

Conversation ceases as you both eat heartily. Finally, with a satisfied sigh, Joseph rises."Please excuse me, friend. I must speak with my captain before we resume our journey," he says with a smile. "He will wish to halt for the day long before I do. No matter how many times I assure him that there are no 'shades of the dead' to walk at night, he refuses to believe me!" Joseph sighs. "I have too far to go to stop so early; there is much work to be done!" With a smile, Joseph steps out of the cabin.

Leaping flames surround you, and you find yourself once again in the chariot.

Decide Your Own Adventure 91

"Now I shall take you back in time again," says the steed quietly. "You will go more than thirteen years into the past, where you may choose between watching Joseph's brothers plot against him, or you may watch them deceiving their father into believing that Joseph is dead. What is your choice?"

Your heart heavy, you realize that you have no wish to see either! You like Joseph already, and cannot imagine what life must have been like for him. To be betrayed by his own brothers, and torn away from everything and everyone he loved—your heart aches for the loneliness and terror he must have endured. Sighing, you realize that you must make a decision.

If you decide to hear
Joseph's brothers' plot, go to page 25.

If you decide to see Jacob being deceived,
go to page 44.

(You Have Decided to See Jacob Send His Sons to Egypt)

"Hurry!" a sharp voice barks in your ear. "They're to leave at sun-up *today,* not tomorrow!" The grizzled old man growling at you tosses you a woolen cloth. You watch carefully as he folds one just like it several times before tossing it over the back of the donkey in front of him.

Your fingers clumsy with haste, you fold the blanket and throw it over the donkey in front of you. The animal's soft brown eyes regard you nervously; he seems to sense that you have never done this before!

Still watching the old man carefully out of the corner of your eye, you place a thick, straw-stuffed pad on top of the blanket; lastly, a fringed and tasseled cloth covers the riding saddle. You move quickly to prepare the next donkey, seeing many others waiting patiently for their loads.

At last you are finished and have time to steal a quick glance at your surroundings. Red fingers of light from the rising sun creep across the brown, dusty earth. Yellowed leaves, shriveled with thirst, hang listlessly on dying trees. The parched dirt is a mosaic of cracks and fissures, and you wonder how long it has been since rain moistened the landscape.

Several men stride briskly out of a large tent nearby. Although they are older and thinner, you recognize Joseph's brothers. Their lean faces are alive with excitement and their eyes sparkle with anticipation. One by one, they respectfully kiss their aged father.

"Never fear, Father," says one of the men, "we will bring home plenty of grain from Egypt."

A youth stands by Jacob's side, looking wistfully at the waiting donkeys. "I wish I were going with you," he says sadly.

Jacob turns to him with a sigh. "No, my son," he says softly. "You know that I am afraid harm will befall you. You are all that I have left of my Rachel, and I want you with me."

"Don't grieve, Benjamin," says Reuben with a sympathetic grin. "We will take note of all the splendid sights of Egypt and faithfully describe every one to you when we return. Perhaps," he adds with a twinkle in his eyes, "we may be able to bring you a gift. So let's have no more sadness, my brother!"

Benjamin smiles gratefully at Reuben. The donkey under your hand moves restlessly, his bridle jingling in his impatience to be off. One of the men approaches this donkey and smiles excitedly.

"Egypt!" he murmurs breathlessly. "Never did I think that I would see the pyramids, and the sphinx, and perhaps, even the court of Pharaoh himself!"

Swiftly, the brothers mount the waiting donkeys. The sun bursts above the horizon, painting tall, thin shadows on the parched ground.

"We'll be back before you know it, little brother," calls one of the men to Benjamin, who is standing dejectedly by Jacob's side. "We'll bring enough grain to fill our bellies at last!"

You look hard at the men's faces, remembering that just thirteen years ago they plotted to kill

Joseph. There is a sadness in their eyes that was not there before, you reflect with satisfaction. *Could it be that they have repented of their wickedness?* Their faces are lined with the cares of middle age now, and hunger has sharpened the contours. You wonder if they ever think about their brother, sold into slavery so many years ago.

With a jingle of bridles, their caravan moves south. Jacob draws Benjamin gently back inside the tent.

The flaming chariot appears on the dusty ground, hiding the caravan from sight. Eagerly, you climb inside, wondering where you will go next.

"You also will journey to Egypt," chimes the low voice softly. "Joseph is now governing Egypt—second in command only to the pharaoh himself. You may join Joseph in his travels on the Nile, or you may go to his villa. Which shall you choose?"

Your heart races with excitement at the thought of seeing ancient Egypt. Either choice sounds fascinating! You swiftly take the reins in your hands, and make your decision.

**If you decide
to join Joseph on the Nile, go to page 87.**

**If you decide to go to Joseph's villa,
go to page 96.**

(You Have Decided to Go to Joseph's Villa)

You find yourself in an airy hall. Soft light filtering in through windows brings a brightly-painted mural to life on the opposite wall. On both sides of the mural, wood columns soar toward the ceiling, ending in the fragile curves of lotus blossoms.

"Come, come!" a sharp voice snaps behind you. "What can you be thinking of to stand there like a stone?"

A firm grasp on your elbow forces you down the long hall, which opens into a vast room. You cast a sidelong glance at the man who propels you. He is an older man, and his manner suggests that he is accustomed to being obeyed.

You step into the huge, high-ceilinged room and stop in amazement. The floor beneath your feet is painted a soft greenish-blue, with life-like painted forms of fish swimming across its glassy surface. The lower edges of the walls are painted with reeds, and ducks so life-like that they seem almost ready to call out. Bright poppies and cornflowers painted on the walls almost wave in the breeze, and you realize in awe that you have never been in such a beautiful room. An intricately-carved chair, its inlaid glass design winking in the soft light, sits in splendid isolation on the low brick platform opposite you.

"I can see that you have not found the senet board," the man scolds. "Run out to the garden—perhaps it was left there!"

He pushes you in the direction of a doorway beside the brick dais; you blink in the glare of sunlight after the shady blues and greens of the room you have just left. You gaze around you in confusion, for you had not expected such a huge garden.

In the distance, vines tumble down high stone walls. Neat stone paths, lined with palms and flowering trees, take off in several directions. You head uncertainly down the nearest path, marveling at the profusion of trees and flowers surrounding you. The path ends abruptly at the edge of a huge, rectangular pool. Lotus blossoms bump each other gently on its surface.

"Are you looking for me, youngster?" asks a soft voice.

Startled, you whirl around to face a tall Egyptian man. Golden bracelets set with flashing stones adorn his strong arms, and an intricate, bejeweled pectoral covers his upper chest. His kohl-lined eyes are kind, and with a jolt you realize that you have found Joseph!

"I am supposed to find the senet board," you stammer awkwardly, wishing that you had some idea what exactly a senet board could be!

Joseph's eyes crinkle in amusement. "That game must have feet, must it not?" he says with a chuckle. "I'm afraid that I am the guilty party—I brought it here last evening. Come!" he smiles. "I think that I remember where I left it."

Together you amble down the smooth stone path, coming at last to a bench set beneath a flowering tree. Soft pink petals shower gently to earth in the breeze, and their delicate scent hovers in the sun-warmed air.

"Here you are, my friend," says Joseph, handing you a smooth, wooden box.

Decide Your Own Adventure

You glance at the box curiously, for you have never seen anything like it before. Three rows of ten squares each cover the top, much like a thin chessboard. A small drawer, not completely closed, reveals a jumble of flattened hour-glass shaped playing pieces, and thin slivers of wood that look like a child's pick-up sticks.

"Would you like to play a short game?" Joseph asks you with a twinkle in his eyes.

As you hesitate, both of you hear hasty footsteps approaching.

"My lord," says the arrival, bowing deeply to Joseph.

"Yes, my faithful Snefru — what is it?" he replies.

The Egyptian's face is creased in a frown. "We have heard that another caravan from Canaan approaches. No doubt they too will wish to buy grain, for I have heard that the drought continues there just as it does here. Do you wish to deal with them yourself?"

Joseph's eyes darken suddenly, and you wonder if every mention of his homeland reminds him of the horror of being sold into slavery so many years ago. The messenger watches him in concern, waiting patiently for the answer.

"Yes, Snefru — I will deal with these Canaanites myself," responds Joseph. He turns to you kindly. "Perhaps later we may have a game, youngster," he says with a smile as he and Snefru stride briskly away. You are wondering if you should follow when the flames of the chariot suddenly blaze before you.

The steed's low, musical voice chimes gently.

"Your choice now is between two events, more than thirteen years into the past. You may watch Joseph's brothers plot against him, or you may watch them deceiving their father into believing that Joseph is dead. What is your choice?"

You reflect unhappily that neither alternative is appealing; you have no wish to see Joseph's wicked brothers again! On the other hand, it would be awful to see Jacob's sorrow. You force yourself to remember your quest, thinking carefully. You take the reins in your hands, and pull them taut.

If you decide to hear Joseph's brothers' plot, go to page 25.

If you decide to see Jacob being deceived, go to page 44.

Decide Your Own Adventure 99

(You Have Decided to See Joseph's Brothers In Pharaoh's Court)

You find yourself in the familiar, cool shadows of the royal audience hall, and glance swiftly at the dais across the room. The handsome, well-built Joseph creates an impressive sight as he supervises the activity in the room. A massive golden necklace cascades down his chest, and the heavy gold signet ring of the pharaoh sparkles on his finger. You realize with a start that his royal bearing and Egyptian clothes make Joseph look exactly like an Egyptian ruler—the only trace of the little shepherd boy from Canaan is the kind and loving expression in his eyes!

A confusion of voices swirls throughout the room, and you look curiously around. Dark-skinned Nubians jostle Midianites, and several languages compete in an uproar of confusion. You catch your breath as you recognize Joseph's brothers approaching the dais, their distinctive tunics setting them apart from the rest of the throng.

You elbow your way swiftly through the crowd, eager to see and hear what happens at this meeting. The last time these men saw Joseph was when they sold him into slavery more than twenty years ago! You hide behind a massive stone pillar only a few feet away from the dais.

Joseph's eyes betray no emotion as he gazes down at his brothers. They approach him nervously, awe and fear etched on their faces. They sink down to their knees before the mighty, Egyptian ruler. One by one, they flatten themselves on the

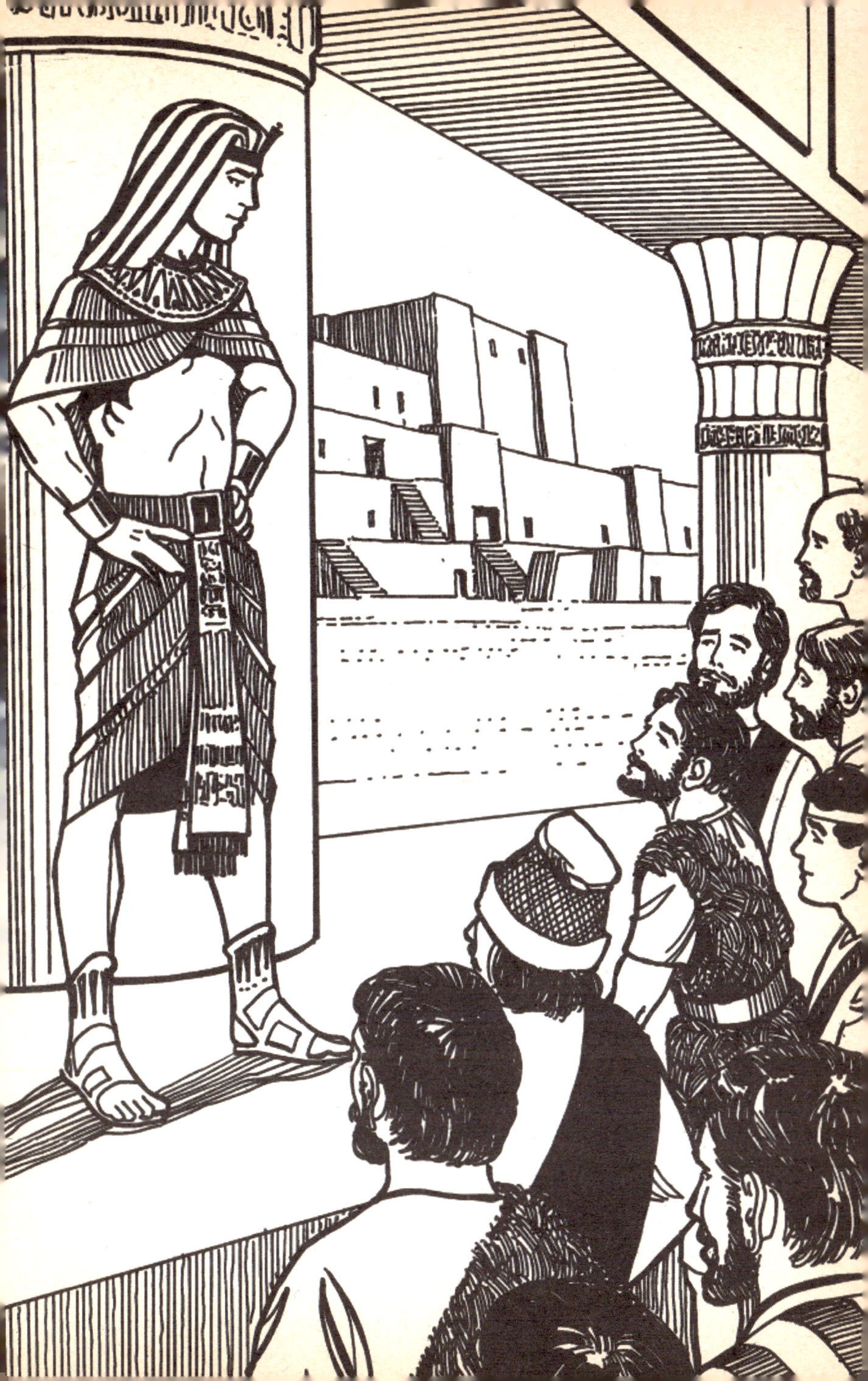

floor at Joseph's feet in the age-old position of submission. At this sight, your heart races—you remember young Joseph's dream that his brothers would bow to him, and here they are!

"They may rise," Joseph says calmly in Egyptian to a servant at his side.

The servant bows slightly, then speaks in Hebrew to the ten men. "You may rise," he translates.

Delighted that you are able to understand both Hebrew and Egyptian, you wonder fleetingly why Joseph is not speaking Hebrew to his brothers, but instead is speaking Egyptian to his interpreter. You shrug inwardly, resolving to puzzle over it later.

Awkwardly, the men rise to their feet, stealing wondering glances at the second most powerful man in Egypt.

"Where have you come from?" Joseph barks harshly. His interpreter hurriedly translates, and the men look uneasy.

"From the land of Canaan," one answers nervously, "to buy food."

"You are spies!" growls Joseph. "You have come to see where our land is unprotected!"

The men's faces drain of color as the servant translates Joseph's words. "No, my lord! Your servants have come to buy food," another answers, his voice trembling. "We are all sons of one man; we are honest men. Your servants are not spies!" he finishes.

Joseph's eyes glitter strangely as he watches his brothers cower before him. "You have come to seek out the undefended parts of our land," he repeats.

"Your servants are twelve brothers in all," another

of the men insists, his voice desperate. "We are the sons of one man in the land of Canaan; and behold, the youngest is with our father today, and one is no more."

Ha! you reflect. *That's what they think!*

Joseph's lips compress into a thin line, and he folds his arms across his chest. The men's faces are fixed in agonizing intensity upon his face — and not one of them recognizes their younger brother. At last, Joseph speaks again, still in Egyptian.

"It is as I said to you, you are spies," he says tonelessly. "And this is how you will be tested: by the life of Pharaoh, you shall not go from this place unless your youngest brother comes here! Send one of you that he may get your brother, while the rest of you remain confined, that your words may be tested, whether there is truth in you. But if not, by the life of Pharaoh, surely you are spies!"

As the translator's voice dies away, a hush falls over the crowd. Every eye is upon Joseph, for even without being able to understand his words, the foreigners present know that the man from whom everyone must buy food is angry. Instantly, several Egyptian soldiers, their swords drawn, surround the Hebrew men. Joseph's brothers are escorted firmly from the room, while the crowd watches in wide-eyed attention.

The scene fades from sight as the flames of the chariot engulf you. Hesitantly you ask, "What happens to them now?"

The steed's voice is soothing as it replies, "They will remain in prison for three days; certainly a much shorter imprisonment than Joseph suffered!"

Decide Your Own Adventure   103

"Then what will happen?" you question.

"You may see for yourself," replies the voice softly. "I am permitted to take you three days forward, to Joseph's brothers' released. Or you may choose instead to visit a remote outpost of the Egyptian frontier, where soldiers are carrying out Joseph's instructions."

The voice falls silent, and you discover with a thrill that you would really like to see Egyptian soldiers at work—when will you ever again have such a chance? On the other hand, you'd like to see what happens after Joseph's ten brothers are released from prison. You take the reins in your hands, and pull them taut.

If you decide to see Joseph's brothers released from prison, go to page 108.

If you decide to go to the Egyptian frontier, go to page 83.

104   Decide Your Own Adventure

(You Have Decided to Join Joseph's Brothers In Prison)

You find yourself once again in the vast, cheerless prison. You know that it has been more than seven years since Joseph was in charge here—and with increasing horror you see the difference without his influence. Years-old cobwebs trail down from the high ceilings, and filth is encrusted on the walls and floor. The light from a single torch gutters hopelessly in the gloom, revealing ten of Joseph's brothers huddled despairingly on the dirty floor.

"How long?" wails one of the men. "What if Pharaoh's second-in-command forgets us down here?"

"This is the third day—and we have heard nothing!" replies another grimly. "How are we to convince him that we are not spies, if he lets us die in prison?"

"We are all guilty," moans another. "Did I not tell you, 'Do not sin against the boy,' and you would not listen? Now comes the reckoning for his blood!"

"Reuben, be still," says one of the men with a frown, although his voice is gentler than his words. "We all know what wickedness we committed against Joseph. His blood is indeed upon our heads! But feeling guilty will not help us down here."

Keys rattle in the rusty lock, and the massive wooden door creaks open. A well-muscled Nubian, his face expressionless, beckons briefly.

"Come!" he says shortly. "Zaphenath-Paneah wishes to see you."

The men scramble to their feet, eager to leave the stale, smelly prison. As the last man leaves the room, the chariot's clean light suddenly throbs in the filthy prison. You scramble quickly aboard, happy to think of leaving.

"Your choice now is between the future and the past," says the steed softly. "You may go forward to Canaan, when Joseph's brothers return from Egypt. Or you may go back in time to the birth of Joseph's

106   Decide Your Own Adventure

brother, Benjamin. You will learn from either choice."

Puzzled, you really don't see how either choice will help you on your quest. You take the reins in your hands, and make your decision.

If you decide to go forward to Canaan, go to page 115.

If you decide to go back to the birth of Benjamin, go to page 17.

Decide Your Own Adventure 107

(You Have Decided to See Joseph's Brothers Released From Prison)

Your heart skips a beat as you find yourself staring up at the turbaned Midianite, his dark eyes flashing in anger. "Watch your manners," he snarls, "and do not even *think* about pushing me again!"

You stammer a hasty apology and his face relaxes. "Look!" he murmurs, pointing toward the back of the room. "Those accursed Canaanites have been released from prison. Perhaps Zaphenath-Paneah is going to have them executed!" he says delightedly, his mouth twisting into a wicked grin.

You shudder as you edge your way cautiously through the crowd away from the bloodthirsty Midianite. Peering around a pillar, you see Joseph's brothers approach the dias, their faces pale with fright.

Joseph rises from the golden throne in the center of the dais, and motions to the interpreter. "Do this and live," he says gently, "for I fear God."

As the translator relays Joseph's message, the men stare at Joseph in amazement. You realize that they are thunderstruck to hear that the second-in-command of mighty Egypt knows and obeys the one true God!

"If you are honest men," Joseph continues, "let one of your brothers remain in prison; but as for the rest of you, go—carry grain for the famine of your households."

Stunned relief mingles with fear on the men's faces, as the translator's voice pauses; who is to remain in prison, and why?

Watching his brothers steadily, Joseph continues. "Bring your youngest brother to me, so your words may be verified, and you will not die," he finishes gently. Tears are streaming down several of the men's faces, as they huddle together at the foot of Egypt's throne.

"Truly we are guilty concerning our brother Joseph, because we saw the distress of his soul when he pleaded with us, yet we would not listen," weeps one. "Therefore this trouble has come upon us!"

You recognize Reuben, his eyes stricken with grief. "Did I not tell you, 'Do not sin against the boy,' and you would not listen?" he wails. "Now comes the reckoning for his blood."

They don't know that Joseph can understand every word they speak! you think, as you cast a swift glance at Joseph. Tears sparkle in his eyes and he turns hastily away from his brothers. At last Joseph looks at his brothers again, his face now empty of expression. He makes a swift gesture to a waiting soldier, who springs into action. Unhooking a stout leather cord coiled against his side, the soldier quickly and efficiently begins binding one of the men.

"Simeon," breathes one of the brothers, his eyes wide as he watches the next-to-the-oldest brother being firmly tied.

You cannot be certain after so many years have passed, but you think you recognize Simeon as the cruelest brother, who seemed the most eager for Joseph to die. The others watch in stunned silence as Simeon is led from the room by armed guards.

Joseph speaks softly to a servant at his side, who

beckons the brothers to follow him. The room disappears as you find yourself once again in the chariot of fire.

"I don't understand," you puzzle aloud. "Why didn't Joseph just come right out and tell his brothers who he was? Why the tricks?"

"Do you not think that Joseph has a right to see if his brothers have changed in twenty years?" asks the steed quietly. "Remember—he has only their word that his brother Benjamin is still alive. Don't you think that he wonders if they have dealt with Benjamin as they did with him so many years ago?"

"Oh, I see!" you exclaim. "Joseph can't know that his brothers are better men unless their actions show it!"

The tinkling chimes of the steed's laughter splinter the silence. "Exactly, little one. Now it is time for your decision. You may join Joseph's brothers on their journey home to Canaan, or you may join Simeon in prison. Which shall you choose?"

You shudder at the thought of seeing the inside of the prison again—and you're not thrilled about being closed up with Simeon, if he is the one you remember. But which choice would help you more on your quest?

If you decide to see the brothers during their journey home, go to page 111.

If you decide to join Simeon in prison, go to page 113.

(You Have Come to See the Brothers During Their Journey Home to Canaan)

Only a sliver of the setting sun remains visible and a sharp black shadow looms before you on the desert sand. Shivering a little, you glance behind you. Silent and unchanging, the sphinx gazes toward the east, its mysterious face empty of expression. Awed, you gaze upward at its immense height until you are startled by a shout that echoes sharply in the twilight.

"My money!" a man cries.

You look around swiftly to see Joseph's brothers busily removing the burdens from their donkeys' backs. One stands open-mouthed, his face pale with fright, beside an open sack of grain.

"My silver has been returned," he stammers. "Here it is in my sack!"

Reuben hurries over, peering anxiously into the sack. "What is this that God has done to us?" he mumbles, as the other men rush to look for themselves.

You puzzle over the reason for their fear. *Why does it matter that the money is in the sack with the grain?* You feel a soft muzzle push gently against your shoulder, and turn to gaze into the gentle, brown eyes of a donkey. One of the men follows, petting the donkey absent-mindedly. "What are we to do?" he murmurs.

"Why do you have to do anything?" you ask boldly.

The man looks at you strangely. "You must know how Egyptians feel about Hebrews," he answers. "They won't even eat at the same table with us!

Decide Your Own Adventure 111

Why would they give us grain and then return our money?" Aware that you must not reveal that this has been Joseph's doing, you are silent.

"There is only one possible reason," he continues, his face grim. "They will say that we are thieves—that we took the grain without paying for it. Then the man will have an excuse to kill us if we return to Egypt!" He hurries away toward the others, the donkey wandering slowly after him.

You cast a look up at the sphinx, looming black against the twilit sky. Dancing white flames suddenly blot the scene from sight, and you find yourself once more in the chariot.

"Your choice now is between two future times," says the familiar voice. "You may go more than four hundred years into the future, to see Moses leading the children of Israel out of Egypt."

How in the world will that help me on my quest? you wonder in amazement.

"Or I may take you to the time of the brothers' second trip to Egypt, where they will be arrested for stealing a silver cup. What is your decision?"

You know that shortly after their arrest, Joseph reveals his true identity to his brothers. On the other hand, it might be interesting to skip forward to the time of Moses, even though you don't understand how that could help. Thoughtfully, you decide.

If you decide to go forward to the time of Moses, go to page 136.

If you decide to see the men arrested for theft, go to page 125.

(You Have Decided to Join Simeon In Prison)

A pair of eyes glitters in the almost-total darkness of the prison. Your nostrils quiver in disgust at the stench of filth, and your foot slips sickeningly on the long-unwashed floor. A low, despairing moan pierces the gloom, and the hair on the back of your neck rises at the sound.

You slip, and fall with a thud on the hard stone floor. The eyes glance at you, apprehensive. Pain shoots up your arm, and you rub your sore elbow gingerly. A low voice speaks from the gloom at last.

"Do you come to torment me?" the voice asks tonelessly.

You shiver at the lifeless voice echoing out of the darkness. "Oh, no!" you answer swiftly.

"Yes, you are here to drive me mad with remorse," says the deep voice. The features of Simeon's face swim into focus as your eyes grow more accustomed to the dark, and you see that his shoulders are slumped in despair.

You can't help feeling pity for this man—although you remember that he showed no mercy to Joseph so many years ago when he wanted him dead! "No, honestly—I'm not here to torment you!" you protest.

After a long, shuddering sigh, Simeon speaks again. "I will die in this prison, you know. Our father will never allow my brothers to bring Benjamin here."

You think for a moment, and then say softly, "But

you don't *know* that he won't. Perhaps your brothers *will* bring Benjamin, and then you'll go free!"

"Never!" he groans. "How could Pharaoh's assistant have known that I, as the oldest when Reuben was absent, was chiefly responsible for Joseph's death? My own guilt has brought my doom! My father will *never* part with Benjamin! Oh, that I could undo the wickedness we did so many years ago!"

Simeon buries his face in his hands and sobs, his shoulders heaving. You stare at him in pity, uncertain what you should say. You almost shout with joy when the pure white flames of the chariot engulf you, and you can see Simeon no more.

"Do not grieve for him," says the voice gently. "There are times when remorse is the best food a soul can have. Now I am permitted to take you to join Joseph's brothers on their journey home to Canaan."

Hoping you will never have to see the inside of the prison again, you take the reins in your hands and wait.

Go to page 111.

(You Have Decided to Go Forward to Canaan)

Dust stings your nostrils as a dry wind whips whirlwinds across the parched, cracked ground. Heat waves shimmer above the nearly lifeless soil, and as far as you look, you see only stunted vegetation. Jacob sits cross-legged in the shadow of his tent, surrounded by nine of his sons.

"Go back to Egypt," quavers Jacob's old voice. "Buy us a little more food."

Judah shakes his head gloomily. "Zaphenath-Paneah solemnly warned us, 'You shall not see my face unless your brother is with you,'" he reports in a low voice. "If you send Benjamin with us, we will go down and buy you food. But if you do not send him, we will not go down!"

The others nod miserably. Jacob's eyes flash, and his lips thin angrily. "Why did you treat me so badly by telling the man that you had another brother?" he wails. "You have bereaved me of my children: Joseph is no more, Simeon is no more, and now you would take Benjamin!"

"How could we possibly know that the man would say, 'Bring your brother down'?" moans one of the brothers.

Judah stirs impatiently, and turns to Jacob. "Send the lad with me," he says firmly, "and we will arise and go—that we may live and not die."

Startled, you realize that the famine really *must* be terrible, if only food from Egypt stands between Jacob's family and death!

"You may hold me responsible for his safety,"

Decide Your Own Adventure

continues Judah. "If I do not bring him back to you and set him before you, then let me bear the blame before you forever. But we have wasted enough time as it is. If we had not delayed, surely by now we could have been there and back— twice!"

The others murmur agreement, and you watch as Jacob wrestles with himself in silence. At last, the old man nods. "If it must be so, then do this: take some of the best products of the land in your bags, and carry them down to Zaphenath-Paneah as a present. Take a little balm, a little honey, aromatic gum and myrrh, pistachio nuts and almonds. And take double the amount of money in your hand, for you must return the silver that was found in your sacks; perhaps it was a mistake."

The brothers, much thinner now than when last you saw them, jump eagerly to their feet. Slowly, Jacob rises. "Take your youngest brother also," he says sadly, "and return to the man. May El Shaddai grant him compassion upon the sight of you, that he may return to me Simeon and Benjamin."

"Come—let us make our preparations swiftly," says Reuben. "We should set out tomorrow at daybreak. I shall tell Benjamin myself that he is to come with us this time!"

Several of the men grin, their eyes flashing with sudden amusement. "He won't be *too* disappointed, will he?" chuckles one.

You see the chariot of fire standing patiently behind the tent, and you slip away quietly to mount behind the steed. As the flames surround you, the musical voice is low in your ear. "I am going to take you back into the past now," says the steed, "to the time of Benjamin's birth."

Puzzling over what you could possibly learn there, you take the reins absent-mindedly into your hands.

Go to page 17.

(You Have Decided to See Joseph's Brothers Speak to the Steward)

You find yourself standing before the imposing stone walls of an Egyptian villa. You catch a glimpse of tall palm trees swaying inside the enclosure, but your attention is immediately drawn to Joseph's brothers, who stand huddled nervously at the gate.

"Why did the honorable Zaphenath-Paneah wish for us to come here," quavers one. "This is his *house!*"

Another brother moans softly. "I don't like this," he says apprehensively. "This is because of the money that was returned in our sacks the first time. We're going to be taken for slaves!"

The gate opens suddenly, and the brothers fall silent as Joseph's steward bows courteously.

"Oh, my lord," Reuben hurries into speech. "We indeed came down the first time to buy food. And it came about that when we arrived at home and opened our sacks, behold, each man's money was in his sack, our money in full! So we have brought it back in our hand."

Reuben halts, draws a breath, and plunges on. "We have also brought down other money in our hand to buy food; we do not know who put our money in our sacks!" he finishes, eyeing the steward fearfully.

The steward's face crinkles into a kind smile. "Be at ease," he says gently. "Do not be afraid. Your God and the God of your father has given you treasure in your sacks; I had your money."

Joseph's brothers appear almost to melt with relief. The steward claps his hands sharply, his eyes twinkling. "And now it is time for a reunion," he says with a grin. "My master has sent word for your brother to be returned to you!"

"Simeon!" shouts Reuben, his face flushed with joy and relief. The brothers embrace and all talk at once. They are overjoyed to learn that they are not to be treated as thieves, and to see Simeon again. One voice carries above the rest. "Did you hear what the steward said?" he questions. "He is an Egyptian—yet he speaks of our God! He said 'your God and the God of your father has given you treasure'!"

Joseph's brothers pause, each face stamped with wonder. They fade from sight as you find yourself back in the chariot.

"You will have no decision this time, little one," says the steed. "Joseph will honor his brothers at a banquet, and then tomorrow they will start home to Canaan with more grain. But just as they leave the city," continues the voice, "they will be arrested for the theft of Joseph's silver cup. I shall take you there now."

Go to page 125.

(You Have Decided to See Joseph's Banquet)

"Don't stand there idle!" snaps a voice in your ear. "Go to the kitchen and bring back a tray. Run!" A red-faced Egyptian deals you a stinging slap between your shoulder blades, and you jog swiftly off in the direction of busy servants.

You scarcely have time to look around as you follow them down cool stone steps and out into a courtyard. Hurrying past beehive-shaped grain silos, you round the corner of the two-story villa. Servants bearing heavily-laden trays hurry out of one of the rooms set against the walls surrounding the villa. You enter the room, to see a scene of frenzied activity.

Delicious aromas mingle temptingly, making your mouth water. An enormous roasted ox is being carried out on the shoulders of several men who strain under the load. Steamed fish are arranged on platters and silver bowls are heaped with plump grapes, pomegranates, and juicy slices of melon. A chubby Egyptian thrusts a silver jug brimming with milk into your hands.

"What are you waiting for?" he pants. "Take this to the table of our honored guests!"

You hustle back across the courtyard, and up the steps into the great hall. At last you have a chance to look at your surroundings. In the cool, corner shadows of the vast room, several musicians play a wandering tune on woodwinds made from reeds. Two long, gleaming, ebony tables face each other across the width of the room. At one of the tables, Egyptian noblemen relax in carved chairs. The other table is empty now, but eleven polished chairs await the arrival of Joseph's brothers. You hurry to hide in the shadow of the carved pillar closest to the empty table, hoping that no one will call you away from your vantage point.

Joseph himself strides into the room and swiftly mounts the steps onto the brick dais. His kohl-lined eyes glitter strangely as he watches his brothers enter the hall. Each man approaches the foot of the dais and, in the age-old custom of respect, flattens himself on the ground before the right hand of Pharaoh. Joseph motions them to rise, and inquires through his interpreter, about their health.

"And is your old father well, of whom you spoke?" Joseph asks, his voice trembling slightly. "Is he still alive?"

"Your servant, our father, is still alive," answers one brother, wide-eyed that this powerful Egyptian would show any interest in their father. "He is quite well."

Joseph's eyes travel from one man to the next, until at last they light upon Benjamin. You remember that Joseph last saw his baby brother when Benjamin was just two years old—and you are not surprised to see sudden tears flood Joseph's eyes. He steps down from the dais, placing a strong arm around Benjamin's shoulders. "Is this your youngest brother, of whom you spoke to me?" he asks in a voice tight with emotion. "May God be gracious to you, my son."

Suddenly, Joseph whirls away from the group; he strides out of the hall as everyone watches in bewilderment. You press farther back into the shadows, watching the brothers whispering uneasily to one another. At last, Joseph returns.

"Serve the meal," he calls to the servants hovering in the doorway.

He moves to the chair at the head of the table and indicates to Reuben that he is to be seated there. One by one, Joseph seats each of his brothers at the table—and you see their faces pale, as they watch Joseph in amazement. *What's the matter with them?* you wonder.

Servants scurry in, bearing platters and bowls. You step forward with your silver pitcher, carefully pouring the cool, foamy milk into Reuben's goblet. You move down the row, filling each goblet. Straining to hear, you just catch Reuben's whispered words.

"How could he know?" Reuben murmurs. "How could the right hand of Pharaoh seat us according to age? We are seated perfectly, from the oldest to the youngest!"

Joseph sits alone at his own table on the dais. The Egyptians are eating with gusto, laughing uproariously. A waiter bends low as Joseph murmurs something in his ear. He straightens, a surprised look on his face—and then takes from Joseph's own table a delicate silver bowl filled with fruit. Hurrying from Joseph's table, the waiter places the bowl before Benjamin.

Joseph is watching his brothers closely, as their youngest brother is honored by food from the gov-

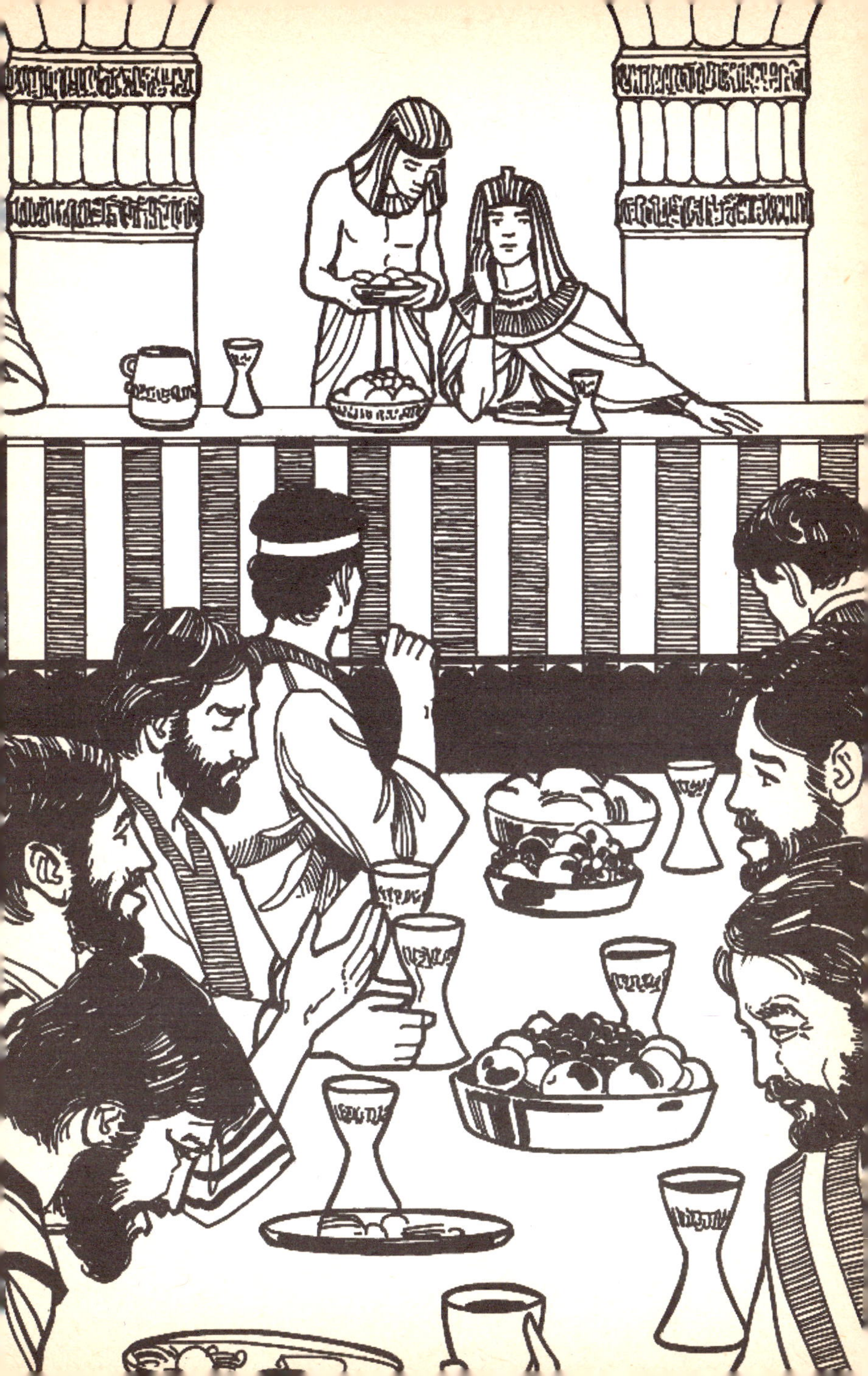

ernor's own table. *He is wondering if they will be angry with Benjamin for being specially honored*, you reflect. The men's fond eyes rest on their youngest brother. Reuben and Judah smile encouragingly at Benjamin, as his eyes grow wide with surprise. Simeon leans forward, calling down to the youngest, "Just think, little brother! What stories you can tell father when we return home!" he chuckles. In amazement, you watch the men tease Benjamin good-naturedly, as Joseph sends platter after platter of special foods from his table to Benjamin. *What a change in all these years!* you think happily. *They hated Joseph for being honored by their father!*

You jump guiltily as you remember that you are supposed to be serving—and your pitcher has been empty for some time. You hurry out of the hall to see the chariot of fire standing silently in the empty corridor. Setting the silver jug carefully down on the stone floor, you climb inside.

"Tomorrow," chimes the steed's voice, "Joseph's brothers will depart for home with the grain that they have bought. But they will be arrested for theft just after they have left the city. That is where I take you now."

Curious, you take the reins in your hands and wait.

Go to page 125.

(You Have Come to See the Men Arrested for Theft)

You find yourself on foot in the midst of a merry caravan. All eleven of Joseph's brothers are leading heavily-laden donkeys away from the city, where obelisks glint in the early-morning sun. Bells on the animals' harnesses jingle merrily, and excitement surges through the group.

"The land of Egypt is filled with wonders," says one happily, "but my heart rejoices to be heading home!"

Benjamin's eyes sparkle. "Won't Father be surprised to hear about the wonderful banquet last night! Imagine—we were the honored guests of the most powerful man in Egypt—next to the pharaoh!"

Simeon twists on his mount, peering back at the city. "Wait!" he says to his brothers, a puzzled frown appearing on his face. "The governor's steward is motioning for us to stop."

The group halts, waiting for Joseph's steward to catch up. Red-faced and panting, he looks at the men reproachfully.

"Why have you repaid evil for good?" he gasps. "Why have you taken the silver cup from which my lord drinks, and which he indeed uses for divination? You have done wrong in doing this!"

The brothers stare at him in obvious confusion. "Why do you accuse us of this?" asks one slowly. "Far be it from your servants to do such a thing!"

The men hastily dismount, each looking hurt and puzzled. Judah faces the steward confidently. "The money that we found in our sacks we have brought back to you from the land of Canaan. Why then would we steal silver or gold from your lord's house?"

Stubbornly, the steward folds his arms across his chest and sets his jaw. Several Egyptian soldiers have joined him now, and they eye the Hebrew men suspiciously.

"With whomever of your servants it is found, let him die," says Judah firmly, his eyes clear and untroubled. "And we also will be my lord's slaves."

Judah's brothers nod agreement, and each hurries to unload bulging sacks from the waiting donkeys. Swiftly, each bag is opened. His mouth grim with determination, the steward begins his search with Reuben's sack. After plunging his arms deep into the grain he appears satisfied— and moves next to Simeon's open bag. Methodically, he searches each sack, until at last he stops in front of Benjamin.

Benjamin's eyes are wide with wonder as the steward bends over his bag of grain. His wonder turns to agony as the steward pulls from his bag an ornate silver cup. With a clash of spears, the soldiers move to surround the youngest, whose face has drained of color. In horror and disbelief, Benjamin stares at the cup.

A wail of desperate grief bursts from Judah's throat, and his clenched fists tear at his robe— your scalp prickles as each brother echoes the terrible wail of grief. The Egyptian soldiers stand uncertainly, waiting for the steward to give them his command. The steward waits, watching the men with an odd expression in his eyes.

He knows they did not steal the cup, you remember as you watch him. *He put it in Benjamin's sack himself, as Joseph instructed him!*

"We will *all* return to the city with you, steward," says Judah, his voice thick with sorrow.

The steward nods briefly, and the scene dissolves in flames as you find yourself back in the chariot.

"Your quest is almost finished, little one," says the steed softly. "Joseph's brothers will return to the city, and Joseph will at last reveal his identity. Do you wish to see their reunion? Or would you like to visit a twentieth century archaeologist on a dig in Shechem, Israel? You may be surprised at what he finds there!"

Torn between the two choices, you make your decision with difficulty.

If you decide to see the dig in Shechem, go to page 141.

If you decide to see Joseph reveal his identity, go to page 128.

Decide Your Own Adventure 127

(You Have Come to See Joseph Reveal His Identity)

You find yourself in a cool, high-ceilinged room. Brightly-painted figures of frogs and ducks almost spring into life on the greenish-blue floor, and the painted reeds low on the surrounding walls almost appear to sway gently before your astonished eyes. Joseph sits silently on a carved chair, and his brothers bow before him. Benjamin's face is white and terrified, and the others surround him protectively.

Judah raises himself from the floor to face Joseph. "What can we say to my lord?" he asks, his voice trembling. "How can we justify ourselves? God has uncovered the guilt of your servants; now we are my lord's slaves, both we and the one in whose possession the cup has been found."

Joseph sits forward slightly in the chair. "Far be it from me to do such a thing," he says softly. "Only the man in whose possession the cup has been found shall be my slave; but as for you, go in peace to your father."

The brothers gasp and Judah steps bravely forward, his jaw set. "Oh my lord, may your servant please speak a word to your ears? Please do not be angry with my boldness, though you are equal to Pharaoh himself."

Joseph nods and his eyes lock with Judah's. Judah begins to speak.

"My lord, this boy, Benjamin, is much loved by his aged father. He is the only remaining son of his mother; his brother is dead. Our father would have refused to let us bring this boy before you, but that all would die unless more food could be brought. With my own life I have promised the safe return of this boy." Joseph's knuckles grow white as he grips the arms of his chair. His face is strained with the effort to hide his emotions. The brothers look on in fear, assuming that the man who holds their lives in his power is growing angry.

"I beg of you, my lord," continues Judah, "let *me* remain as your slave in place of the boy; I cannot return to my father unless the boy is with me, for the grief would bring his gray head to his grave."

Joseph leaps from his chair, knocking it to the floor with a clatter. "Have everyone go out from me!" he commands in Egyptian. "Only these Hebrews may remain!"

Astonished servants scurry from the room, their expressions full of bewilderment and concern. You press yourself nervously against a pillar—hoping that in the shadows you will not be noticed. Tears are flowing down Joseph's cheeks, and a heart-rending wail is torn from his throat.

"I am your brother Joseph!" he sobs in Hebrew. "Then my father is still alive?" Blank, astonished faces stare back at him.

"Please," pleads Joseph, his voice choked with emotion, "come closer to me."

Nervously, the men stumble awkwardly to their feet and approach the dais slowly.

"I am Joseph, whom you sold into Egypt," he says, watching his brothers' awed faces. "And now, do not be grieved or angry with yourselves for selling me here, because it was to save lives that God sent me ahead of you."

Decide Your Own Adventure

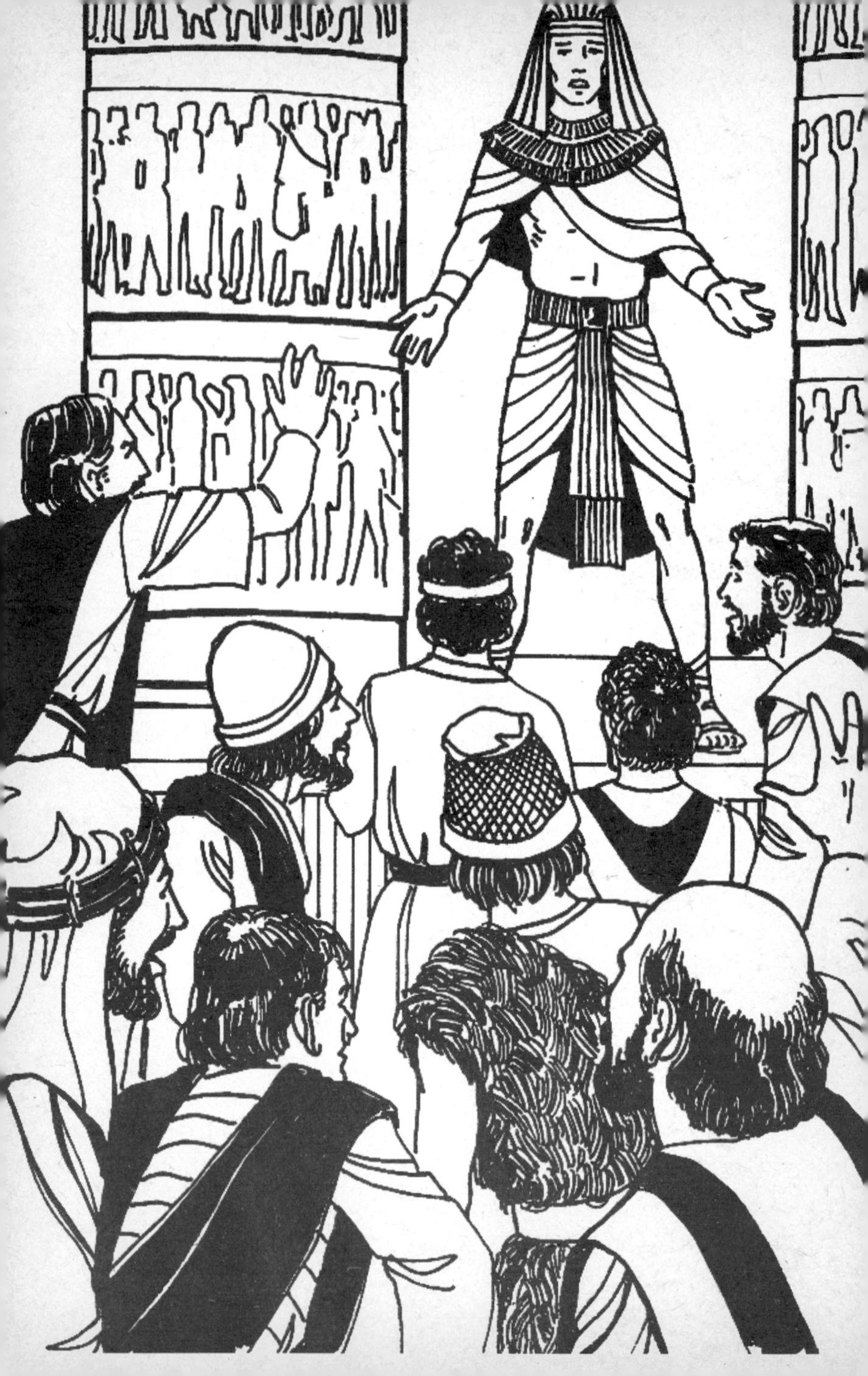

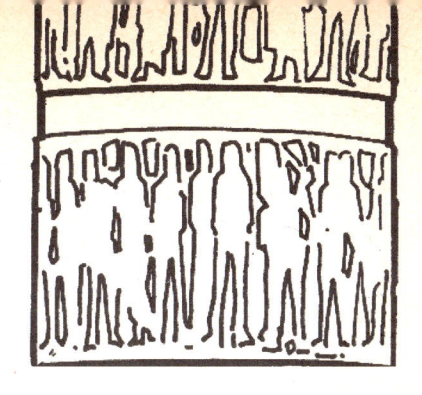

Chills race up and down your spine as you hear Joseph speak. *He asks them not to be sorry they sold him into slavery!* you think in awe. *For over twenty years he has been separated from his father and his beloved land — and he tells them not to grieve!*

Joseph plunges into the midst of his brothers and as he speaks, you watch remorse struggle with joy on their faces.

"It was not you who sent me here, but God," explains Joseph, "and He has made me a father to Pharaoh, lord of all his household, and ruler over all the land of Egypt. Now hurry back to my father and say to him, 'Thus says your son Joseph, "God has made me lord of all Egypt; come down to me, do not delay."'"

The brothers are weeping now, and you begin to think that their reunion should be private. You slip quietly from your place of hiding through the shadows to the nearest door, and find yourself suddenly back in the chariot.

Marveling at the forgiveness you have just seen, you reflect a little sadly that your quest must be over. You have already learned that Joseph was unjustly accused — like Jesus Christ. And like Jesus, he was hated for no reason by his own people. Joseph was like Daniel because both were prisoners in a strange land, and both were given the interpretations of a king's dreams by God. The quiet voice of your steed interrupts your thoughts.

"You are not quite finished, little one. You have learned well, but there is still one more lesson for you to grasp on this journey.

"After Joseph revealed himself to his brothers, they returned to Canaan to collect their father, all of their families, and all of their belongings, and returned to Egypt to live under Joseph's care. Now, more than seventeen years into the future, Jacob has died. After burying him in Canaan, as he requested, Joseph and his brothers returned to Egypt to live. I take you there now, to visit with Joseph."

Sad that your quest is almost over, you take the reins in your hands.

Go to page 133.

(After Jacob's Death)

Water-lilies bob gently on the surface of a deep blue pond. Flowering shrubs fill the air with delicate scents, and the brush of palm leaves swaying in the soft breeze mingles with the sound of water trickling from a fountain. On a stone bench in the shadows near the pond's edge, sits Joseph, deep in thought. Older now, his face is lined and his shoulders a little bent. The same gentle eyes are gazing at the pond. Hesitating to disturb the deep peace of this garden, you stand quietly.

Suddenly, Joseph looks directly at you. With a kind smile, he beckons you to sit beside him on the bench. You join him, and wait.

"Are not the ways of God marvelous, my friend?" he asks softly.

A question burns inside you, but you press your lips together firmly; you are determined *not* to ask it.

Joseph's eyes twinkle, and he puts a friendly arm around your shoulder. "Why do you frown so fiercely?" he asks with a chuckle. "I can see that something is troubling you. What is it?"

"Well," you hesitate, "I guess I have two questions." The words tumble out now. "How could you forgive your brothers? They would have killed you if not for Reuben! And they might just as well have killed you when they sold you into slavery!"

Joseph's grey eyes darken, as he gazes beyond the stone walls of the garden. "How could I *not* forgive them?" he says softly. "Am I in God's place? Just look at the good that God brought from their

Decide Your Own Adventure . 133

wicked deed! My whole family was spared death from famine—all because my brothers sold me into slavery!"

"But you were in slavery for so many years!" you protest. "Didn't you ever think that God had forgotten you?"

Joseph stands, a smile playing softly on his lips. "What is time, my friend?" he asks gently. "Do you think that the God of Abraham, Isaac, and Jacob is limited by time?"

"Well, no—of course not," you reply, a little crossly.

"If the Lord God had chosen to rescue me immediately and restore me to my family—how then would I have learned to trust in Him? It is when we are in terrible trouble that we learn about walking with God. What a blessing it is to learn such a lesson!"

"I think I see," you falter. "Sometimes we forget God when everything is going well."

Joseph nods vigorously, and asks again, "What is time to the Lord God? His purpose is far beyond our ability to understand, for He holds eternity in His hand! Just think!" he exclaims, getting up to pace in excitement. "How privileged we are to be taught to forgive those who wrong us!"

With a gasp, you realize that *forgiveness* is the main reason that Joseph is sometimes called the foreshadow of the Savior! *Jesus will forgive even those who put Him to death!* you think in awe.

Joseph sighs gustily. "One day," he says with a smile, "God will bring His children back to the land which He promised on oath to Abraham, to Isaac, and to Jacob."

You think wonderingly of the more than four hundred years from now until Moses delivers the children of Israel from bondage. Then, in another four hundred years, David will become king of Israel—and a thousand later, the Savior will come. You see that God's purpose moves throughout history, while events—both small and great—shape ten thousand tomorrows. Feeling very small and insignificant, you find yourself engulfed by the leaping flames of the chariot as Joseph fades from your sight.

"Remember, little one," says the voice gently, "humble as you may be—you were redeemed by God Himself. His purpose will be fulfilled in your life, as it was in Joseph's."

You know that your journey is now over, and you reluctantly take the reins in your hands. You will not soon forget the lessons you have learned on this journey about humility, forgiveness, and faith in God. Nor will you ever forget the great and gentle Joseph.

THE END

(You Have Decided to Go Forward to the Time of Moses)

The rosy glow of many cheerful fires lights a flat, fertile landscape as far as you can see. Hundreds of tents stretch for miles beneath the black, velvet sky—and excited Hebrews cluster around every fire.

"Here!" a voice shouts gustily. "You, boy! Give us a hand with this!"

A firm hand grasps your elbow, none too gently, and spins you around. "Catch hold of the corner, youngster," puffs a burly man, sweat streaming down his face. He raises his hand to steady a large wooden object resting on his shoulder, as two other men struggle under the same burden. You spring quickly to take hold of the unattended corner, and the burly man groans with relief.

"Ah—that's better. It is difficult to balance, with only three of us. Respectfully, now!" he says sharply, "These are Joseph's bones we carry, remember!"

Excitement surges through your veins, as you eye the wooden coffin as best you can. "Really?" you gasp in wonder. "Is this truly Joseph's coffin?"

"Truly so!" answers the man with a smile. "Joseph made the sons of Israel swear solemnly that they would carry his bones with them when they left Egypt. Don't let this heathen coffin fool you—it's Joseph, alright!"

The man leads the four of you into his own large tent and directs, "Here—set it down gently!"

Straining to lower the heavy coffin carefully, one

of the other men looks at the owner of the tent suspiciously and asks, "Why do you want this thing in your tent?"

The burly man casts an impatient look at him. "Because Moses asked *me* to make certain that Joseph's bones are carried safely to the promised land," he answers curtly.

The two men scurry quickly away, and you and the burly man step out of the tent also. He sits heavily down by the fire, politely motioning you to do the same. The crackling fire makes the painted coffin sparkle eerily in the darkness of the tent behind you.

"What a marvel!" sighs the man happily, gazing into the sky. "Imagine! The promise to Abraham fulfilled to the very day!"

You stare at him blankly. "The promise to Abraham?" you repeat, not understanding what he is talking about.

"Of course!" he thunders, slapping you on the back in a friendly manner. "Surely you know about the promise the Lord God gave to Father Abraham! Have you not heard that his descendants would be as numerous as the stars of the heavens, that they would be strangers in a land not their own for 400 years, part of which time they would be oppressed and enslaved? "

"Y-y-yes," you stammer.

"And," he continues, his voice throbbing with wonder, "that in the fourth generation of life in that strange land, God would bring Abraham's descendants back to Canaan?"

You nod silently.

Decide Your Own Adventure

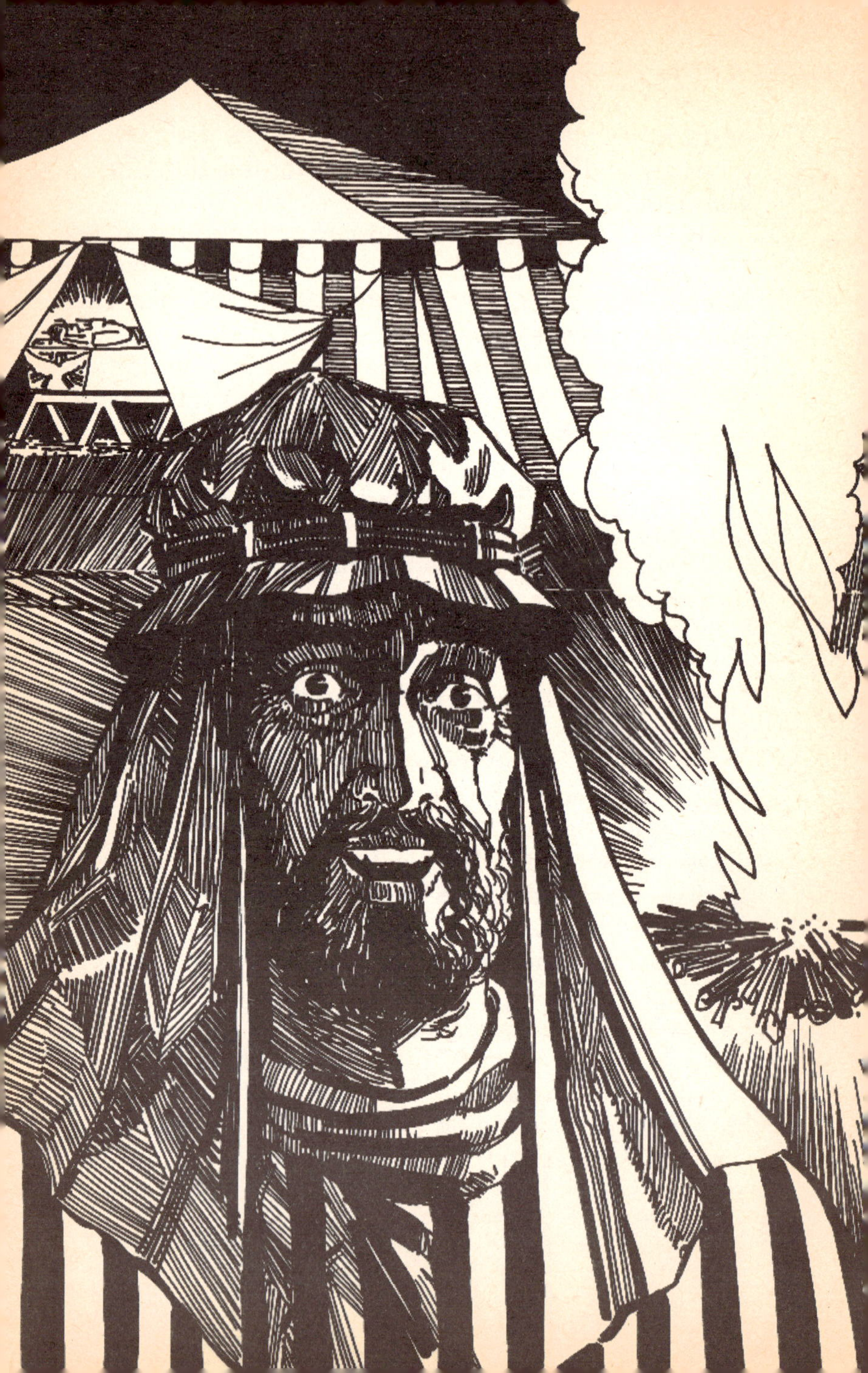

"Joseph and his brothers were the first generation to live in Egypt," the man says swiftly. "Joseph's brother Levi had a son, Kohath. Kohath was the second generation. Kohath's son was Amram, the third generation. And Amram had two sons—the fourth generation. Do you know who Amram's two sons are?" the man's voice has risen in excitement, until he is almost shouting with delight.

Startled, you whisper, "Moses and Aaron?"

"Precisely!" the man answers, his wide face wreathed in smiles. "The fourth generation in Egypt *is* leading us back to Canaan—*and we left 400 hundred years to the day from the time that the Lord's promise to Abraham began to be fulfilled in the birth of his son, Isaac!*" Triumphantly, he leans forward to watch your reaction.

Amazement washes over you as you realize the significance of this clear fulfillment of prophecy. Chuckling, your host ducks inside his tent and you see a throbbing white glow behind it. Springing to your feet, you walk thoughtfully toward your chariot of fire. You cast one last look at the tents of the children of Israel spread beneath the soft black sky; hundreds, thousands, tens of thousands, all descendants of Father Abraham.

After Joseph's death, Egypt was invaded by a foreign government and was ruled by a king who did not know—or care—about Joseph and his people. He knew only that the Hebrews were multiplying quickly and he considered them a threat, so he began to abuse them in terrible ways, hoping to kill them. When this didn't seem to be slowing the

Decide Your Own Adventure

growth of the Hebrew people enough, the king demanded that the Hebrew midwives kill all the newborn baby boys. It was into this situation that Moses, one of the fourth generation of Hebrews was born in Egypt. And now he was leading God's people out of bondage and into the promised land. You shudder at the awesome surety of God's holy Word as you climb into the chariot.

"Time to go back now," the steed's voice is gentle. "I shall take you back to Joseph's time. Joseph's brothers returned to Canaan with the grain they bought from him—but the grain ran out, and still the terrible famine continued. They have returned to Egypt, to buy more— only *this* time, they have brought Benjamin with them. I take you now to join Joseph's brothers as they speak with his steward."

Go to page 118

140   Decide Your Own Adventure

(You Have Decided to See the Dig in Shechem)

A blistering sun beats mercilessly down on your uncovered head. An excited shout erupts behind you, and you whirl around to see a group of turbaned workers cluster around a lean, tanned figure beneath a makeshift tent. You hurry down the hillside, your feet slipping on pebbles, to arrive breathless at the side of the tent.

"Look at this!" the lean man shouts, his leathery face crinkling into a delighted grin. Flinging his pith helmet into a corner of the tent, he wipes a huge bandanna across his glistening forehead. "You all agree, don't you?" he asks urgently, his eyes boring into the faces of the workmen surrounding him. "The tomb where we found this has been reverenced by your people for centuries as the tomb of Joseph?"

Wait a minute! you think, your mind racing. *This is Shechem, on the West Bank of Israel—how could Joseph's tomb be here, when he died in Egypt?*

The archaeologist suddenly points a bony finger at you accusingly, his blue eyes flashing in his brown face. "A-ha! I see a skeptic! Why do you think that this cannot be Joseph's tomb?"

Embarrassed, you answer, "Joseph died in Egypt, didn't he?"

The workmen politely hide their smiles behind gnarled hands, but the archaeologist roars with laughter. "Of course he died in Egypt, youngster! And how would he have been buried?"

You think rapidly that since Joseph was the

Decide Your Own Adventure

second most powerful man in Egypt, he would have been given an almost royal funeral. "Well," you begin thoughtfully, "he would have been mummified, right? Like all important Egyptians were . . . ?"

"Absolutely correct!" the man beams his approval. "And what material would have been used to build his coffin?"

You seem to remember that the Egyptians used wooden coffins, painted on the narrower head end. "Wooden?" you ask hesitantly.

Nodding, the archaeologist's eyes narrow in anticipation. "Now think!" he whispers. "Where did Joseph wish to be buried?"

Desperately, you rack your brains—until suddenly you remember. "In Canaan!" you shout delightedly. "He made his family promise that when they left Egypt, they would take his bones to the land that God had promised to Abraham, Isaac, and Jacob!"

His smile spreading from ear to ear, the man nods vigorously. "Of course!" he exclaims. "And that is why, when Moses led the children of Israel out of bondage, he brought the coffin of Joseph with him!"

"But wait!" you protest. "Moses never set foot in the promised land. What happened to Joseph's coffin?"

His eyes sparkle merrily. "Joshua took over the leadership, and led the Hebrews into Canaan. It was Joshua who buried the bones of Joseph—and the Bible even tells us where!"

"Shechem?" you question eagerly.

"Absolutely!" he answers, grinning. "Now take a

Decide Your Own Adventure 143

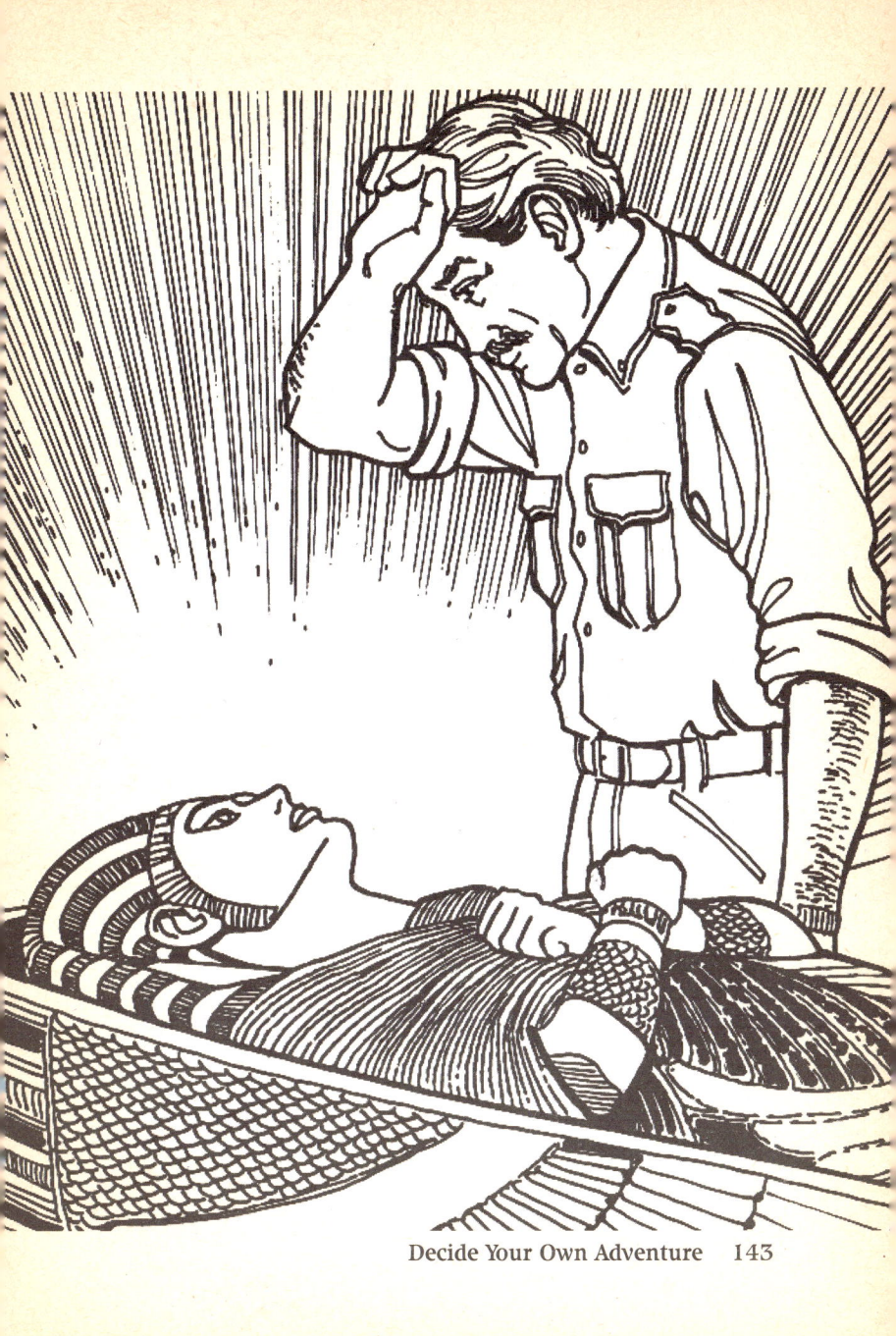

look at what we have found in the very cave that these people have believed was Joseph's burial place for centuries!"

With a proud flourish, the archaeologist whisks a burlap sheet from an object in the center of the makeshift tent. Gooseflesh ripples down your spine as you find yourself staring at an ancient wooden coffin. Your eyes glance quickly over the mummified remains inside, to light on an ornate sword.

"The sword..." you breathe.

The archaeologist's voice is scarcely above a whisper as he answers, "It is indeed an Egyptian nobleman's sword, my friend. Here, in the very spot where the Bible tells us we should find the bones of Joseph, we find exactly what we should find! And some critics say that the Bible is nothing but folklore!" he snorts.

He bends lovingly over the coffin, running his rough hands gently over the ancient wood. The workmen stare, transfixed, at the object—their dark eyes wide with wonder. No one notices you slip away to the waiting chariot.

"You have no decision to make this time," chimes the gentle voice. "I shall take you back in time now, and you shall see Joseph reveal his identity to his brothers. Mark well what you shall learn."

Your thoughts still spinning from what you have just seen, you take the reins in your hands.

Go to page 128.